Change of Address

Change of Address

2005

Poems	Author
New and Selected	**David R. Slavitt**
	Publisher
	Louisiana State University Press
	Baton Rouge

DESIGNER: Barbara Neely Bourgoyne
TYPEFACE: Whitman, text; Franklin Gothic, display
PRINTER AND BINDER: Thomson-Shore, Inc.

Library of Congress Cataloging-in-Publication Data
Slavitt, David R., 1935–
  Change of address : poems, new and selected / David R. Slavitt.
      p. cm.
  ISBN 0-8071-3003-6 (cloth : alk. paper) — ISBN 0-8071-3004-4 (pbk. : alk. paper)
  I. Title.
PS3569.L3C48 2005
811'.54—dc22

2004023917

The paper in this books meets the guidelines for permanence and durability of
the Committee on Production Guidelines for Book Longevity of the Council on
Library Resources. ∞

Contents

Acknowledgments

Some of the new poems have appeared in the *Hudson Review, New Criterion, Poetry,* and the *Harvard Review,* and the author is grateful to the editors of those publications. *Suits for the Dead* was published by Charles Scribner's Sons as a part of their Poets of Today series. *The Carnivore* was published by the University of North Carolina Press. *Vital Signs: New and Selected Poems* was published by Doubleday & Co. The remaining collections were published by Louisiana State University Press. The author is grateful to all of them.

For the nine, the three,
and the one, with love.

New Poems

Change of Address

1

In the still of the night, the works of a quartz clock
advancing the sweep second-hand make the sound of a child
in the next room, bored or mischievous, stupidly
popping bubble wrap and, as he turns real,

my patience, never great, dwindles, exhausted,
but the guise of the god of time reveals itself—
a relentless, destructive brat given to tantrums,
whom it's prudent (but also torture) not to confront.

The walls of the house meanwhile, grown soft and gummy,
would, if I pressed my palms against them, give way
or, like mozzarella, yield to a finger's persistent
probing. I know this, having learned to distrust
what the senses report, for empiricism yields,
as it would to faith, to desperation and panic.

2

Desire is always for something other, later
and elsewhere, abstracting the here and now as it hurries
and harries us into a future we are too shrewd
to suppose will be an improvement. Meanwhile, rot

sets in and the present's rich presence pales,
diminished as if by a doctor's report—there is never
a reckless mention of "cure" but a temporization,
that "five-year survival" in which time changes

its flow, no longer a placid stream but a rush,
a race of white water with eddies and roaring
falls we knew were there but behaved as if
that deadly current had nothing to do with us.
This bed, I can feel, is floating. I try to hold on
to a piling or branch overhead, compiling lists.

3

Motion came later: our earlier order was fixed,
the life of plants to which we return each night
burrowing into the bedding as if to take root
and resume, at least for a time, a vegetative

condition we never forgot. What we call the love
of place is our sense of connection rootlets absorb
with the pungent nutrients only that loam and that water
offer. That geologic concinnity's taste

is what we know and who we are. Transplanted,
we may, elsewhere, survive if not quite thrive,
but at night, for months, for years, the neuron-fine
filaments still will stretch forth in search of terrain
they recognize, the marrow, the special tang
by which we bloomed, vivid still in our dreams.

4

In strangers' rooms, empty or full of their stuff,
you look not merely for housing but what might be right
as the lair of a possible self, that furtive creature
the merest sign of which would give you hope.

Most of the time, what you see are displays of ruin—
why else would they decamp and move on? But now
and again, you have a sense of his having been there,
or even of his impending entrance, proposing

what you for an instant consider and then, for whatever
reason, reject. And you drive off with the agent,
leaving him there in those empty, gloomy rooms
to languish. You're right and feel relief but also
distress for that stillborn wraith you recognized
with his claim of kinship from which you turned away.

5

And then you find that plausible place, the space,
the location, the light, the things that can't be changed,
just what you wanted, but . . . what are they asking? Sordid
questions we put to ourselves about money and time.

But the market is not what I know about, and the experts'
advice is only advice: it is in our guts
that we choose to take the plunge or not. Can we hope
to find something else at that price anywhere as good?

It's stress, and I'm wide awake before dawn and making
plans—to avoid the larger task of deciding,
which happens all by itself. We feel plates shifting
of what we supposed was solid ground, and the shape
of the landscape is different. Do you know you are falling
in love or only realize that you have fallen?

6

And the house that was your house, whose spaces you'd learned,
your accurate hand reaching out for a light switch, your sure
feet counting its steps with no need to trouble
your head: in an instant it's different, a burden you barely

bear. And that you are the one who has been unfaithful
only makes matters worse, for it keeps its silence,
a wronged wife who knows it would do no good
to complain. But her silence accuses. You also suspect

these rooms, even now, may be letting themselves imagine
other, better furniture, pictures, hangings,
and livelier conversations, and surely better
and more attentive cleaning and gardening. Houses,
having their own lives, and with longer spans,
like the long odds and can play a waiting game.

7

We live in our heads mostly but not altogether,
and at moments like this we have to own up to the choices
we seem to have made—appliances, furniture, clothing,
the clutter and junk of a life, much of which we're discarding

with regret, relief, or, after a while, just numbness.
And whatever remains will get packed and put in a van
that is not—I keep telling myself—an enormous hearse,
which is why they are not preceded by flower cars.

Still, what's a house but a resting place? That this one
has not turned out to be my next-to-last
from which they carry me out is no small surprise.
The ancient olive trees, budding once more
and leafing, feel a bit foolish; how much more absurd
is the staff of legends that, stuck in the ground, blossoms.

Kindertotenlied

The frounyng fates have taken hence
Calimachus, a childe
Five yeres of age: ah well is he
from cruell care exilde:
What though he lived but little tyme,
waile nought for that at all:
For as his yeres not many were,
so were his troubles small.

—LUCAN: TIMOTHE KENDALL, 1577, TRANS.

A nice enough conceit, let us agree, but I dare you:
go and put that up in the hallway of Children's Hospital
where some bereaved parent will show you what frounyng is,
if he doesn't deck you.

The poem is not intended for grieving parents;
rather, it may invite us to pretend to such a loss
so as to imagine the stoic wisdom with which to withstand it.
None of us will have that when the terrible moment comes,
and one way or another, believe me, it will come.
But it is flattering to suppose how, on that black day,
we may carry ourselves well,
and the poet's business here is to flatter.

Or Kendall's business, I suspect, was to flatter.
Lucan may have meant it straight,
in the way Aeschylus and Sophocles meant it when they said
what is best is never to have been born.
We are greedy for life and for time,
even knowing what wretchedness they bring.

I stare ahead into the middle distance,
and what I see is a blur
now that my myopia is increasing.
That's bad enough, but it may be a prodrome
of cataracts, which there is no way to prevent.
It is not a prospect worth my squinting to try to see more clearly.

A child who died in his fifth year would be spared this,
but we would not envy him.
We love the light for which the shades in Hades are said to mourn.
And the death of a child seems to be an especially terrible thing,
outrageous and unfair, as if there were ever anything fair about illness and death.

Young animals die all the time,
and famine and plague seize first upon the young and the old,
who are the weak ones.
We may try to understand the logic of this,
but we cannot endorse it.

The poets were not fools and must have shared our assumptions.
The epitaph, then, may have been ironic,
an expression of yearning for the wisdom no man has,
or no man with whom we should want to break bread.

Waile nought for the child?
Ah, but waile, waile for the world
in which such things happen, in which children die.

Waile, too, for those who do not grieve
because they have grasped the stinging nettle of the truth
and it has numbed them.

Blessed are those who mourn,
because they can.

Dust Mites

My granddaughter is allergic to dust mites.
I am sorry to hear this news, but also pleased,
for I approve of her refinement. These are nasty-looking creatures, relatives of
    ticks and spiders,
and they live on flakes of our dead skin, which is disgusting. Nina's little body
    is quite right to take offense.
It is not, strictly speaking, the dust mites themselves to which she is allergic,
but the dust-mite droppings and the dead dust mites. It's the enzymes they use
    to digest skin flakes.
Those of us who are not allergic to this are unspeakably crude.
Her allergy is thought to be related to infantile eczema and to asthma, or at any
    rate is more common in those who have these diseases, or whose relatives
    have them.
My father had asthma. I had infantile eczema. We have a kind of claim, then,
    on Nina's delicacy and refinement.
So, if I am sorry to hear that she has this trouble, I am also proud of her.

Among the suggestions her doctor made was that her stuffed animals should be
    reduced to two, which she is to trade off, a week at a time.
One is to be in bed with her, and the other is to be in a plastic bag in the
    freezer.
The eggs can withstand the cold, but they hatch in a week, and then the little
    beasties die.
When teddy comes out of the cold, fuzzy dog goes in.
My hope is that these animals may learn to survive this peculiar regimen, a
    week in the bed and then a week in the frozen darkness.
And my hope beyond that, which I barely allow myself to frame in words, is
    that Nina may learn from her animals, may pick up somehow their ability to
    get through cold dark times,
never losing hope that there will eventually be a rescue, a reversal, a release, a
    return to the warm bed of the dear little girl at the center of their universe.

Pussy Cat, Pussy Cat

Pussy cat, pussy cat,
where have you been?
I've been to London to see the Queen.
Pussy cat, pussy cat,
what did you there?
I saw a little mouse under her chair.

Ah, pussy cat, are you then altogether unmoved by our ceremonies and pretensions?
Did the queen's majesty mean nothing to you?
Were the splendors of the court beyond your comprehension or beneath your notice?
Are we to understand that mouse you saw as vulnerability or imperfection,
or some sordid truth that we conspire to ignore
(mortality for instance), or what?

Pussy cat, pussy cat
doesn't bother to answer. What on earth for?
Explications are not what she stalks.

In some versions of the nursery rhyme,
the penultimate line has her frighten the little mouse under the chair,
which is quite different, suggesting that each of us has a role to play,
that for anyone, in whatever station in life, there may be an opportunity to serve,
a function in some divine plan . . .

Pussy cat, pussy cat, curled up at the foot of the bed,
has no comment.
Reassurance is what she neither requires nor offers.
She may on occasion deign to play with a catnip toy,
but to the devout theology is not interesting.

Intruder

He broke in, picking the lock, or having stolen
a key, and he knew the code to disarm the alarm,

some homeless guy, a crazy street-person, harmless
you'd think, but you're wrong: he likes it here, and he stays.

He rummages through my closets and dresser drawers
and tries on my clothing, which happens, of course, to fit him.

He runs my comb through his hair. He uses my toothbrush.
He lies down on my side of the bed for a nap.

He has settled in. In the mornings, he sits at my place
and has his coffee and toast, reading my paper.

He borrows my car and drives to meet my classes;
during my office hours he meets with my students.

We don't look at all alike, but he's living my life.
I try to signal my friends with whom he dines

or my wife with whom he is sleeping: "This isn't me.
He's an impostor. How can you not have noticed?

He's old! He's nasty. Also, he's clearly crazy!
How can he fool you this way? And how can you stand him?"

They pay me no mind, pretending not to have noticed.
Could they somehow be in on this together?

But what is his purpose? Was he also displaced
from apartment, job, and wife? Did that turn him desperate?

And must I go out now myself to find a victim,
break into his house, and begin living his life?

Eden

The velvety leaves with their greens tending off toward purple,
the flowers' fragrant profusion, the twittering birds'
erratic darting overhead, the purling
brook . . . these were all trucked in to approximate
what we should like to remember. It wasn't like that.
There was never a garden; he wasn't cast out: he merely
grew up a little, looked around, and sinned,
if you want to call it a sin, by looking harder

at what there was. He tried to be brave, to settle,
but grief is hard to live with, and dismay
unsettles even the best of us. We speak
of a garden, then, to try to console one another
for the riches and ease we insist we've lost, preferring
that to admitting our lives were always poor.

Mars

Mars is of no great interest to me. The question
is not whether there's life out there but whether
life here is anything we can understand,
or stand. The approach from time to time of the red

planet to ours is not compelling enough
to tempt me out to the yard at night to look up
and try to see for myself. But the helpful hint
resonates nonetheless: if you want to see Mars'

redness, you have to peer through a cardboard tube,
an empty paper-towel roll (or toilet-paper
will do almost as well). It blocks out light
from other stars to let the retina's cones

collect and transmit more of the planet's color.
In science's march toward progress, who discovered
this? Not some NASA or Cal Tech hotshot
or desperate drudge in the labs of Scott or Charmin,

but a child, out there at night at his father's side.
The father held his telescope up to his eye
and the little boy or girl with the tube did likewise
to discover it isn't just pretend but works,

making the red redder, and showed the father,
insisting he look, and only to humor the child,
he did, and was even more amazed than the child,
in the light of the years of his life, having been blinded

to how some wishes come true or, say, some prayers
are answered. The child was aware of the difference, was only
pretending, playing, but when the planet comes near,
unless there is play somewhere to which we pay

attention, the god for whom it is named will glower,
and Phobos and Deimos, its moons we cannot see
through any cardboard tube, will loose their fear
and panic upon us all that we shall deserve.

Dying Bird

John Crowe Ransom wrote of death
as a child encounters it in "Janet Waking,"
where the little girl's hen dies, and, her heart breaking,
kneeling, she weeps as fast as she has breath.

It is a minor but stately ode,
restrained and elegant, one of those well-made
pieces I studied in school—I forget in what grade—
by which I was introduced to the pastoral mode,

economical, witty, and small,
or so we think, until we get to the last
line and death's "forgetful kingdom," vast
enough, we realize, to include us all.

Mr. Ransom is dead now, who
published a poem of mine many years ago.
(Cleanth Brooks had told me to send it, and so
I did, and it appeared in the *Kenyon Review*

as my debut.) This all came back
in a rush yesterday, when I was walking downtown
on my way to visit the dentist, and I saw on the ground,
as if it were roosting there, a brown and black

bird in a doorway on Arch Street,
an immature herring gull, wounded or sick,
but unmoving, helpless, down there in the thick
of the passers-by and our indifferent feet

a block from Filene's. My
appointment called, but the sight persisted all day
of that bird's inhuman indifference, or dare one say
acceptance. Its bright, pitiless raptor's eye

could see what was ahead—slow
starvation or sudden attack of stray dog or cat.
Could its life high in the air have brought it to that
heartless assent I study but do not know?

Mr. Ransom's poem implies this
as "Bells for John Whiteside's Daughter" does, too,
but only years after your classroom reading do you
begin to apprehend what the subject is—

grief, and how faith or wisdom can teach
such perfect poise, even there in a busy street,
that takes what comes with the next breath and heartbeat,
as gracefully as on some secluded beach.

Homage to Catatonia

I have glimpsed from the lip of the pit
those artists of motionlessness,
who meditate on the distress
that froze them there, and they sit

breathing shallowly, slowly
melding their minutes to hours,
defying vicissitude's powers,
mad, but quite possibly holy.

In times of danger we flee
or, cornered, may stand and fight.
Or like the opossum hold quite
still and appear to be

dead, or transported elsewhere.
The mind having closed down,
the body is left to its own
devices and melts into air,

or joins in its rhythmic flow
that soothes the spirit's hurts
while the modest flesh reasserts
the truths we'd forgotten we know.

As the organs play, each cell
performs its prescribed rite,
and in comfort or even delight
we can sense how all will be well.

A quirk of the frontal lobe?
Or chemical? But this
endorses the world that is
dysfunctional, too, as Job

and Oedipus understood.
The patients' retreat to trance
could as well represent an advance,
and it does less harm than good.

Desire, ambition, and will
are merciless masters that goad
us who scurry their dusty road,
but heaven is sitting still.

Sestina

The trick is this ordering into relentless rows
of the tangle of words, like plants in a garden, the work
having less to do with the hungry mind than the eye—
surfeited though it may be—which yet has the right
also to be indulged, sometimes and in part,
and for its sake, who would not aspire? I strain

but try to hide the effort it costs to constrain
and display, as the flimsy trellis does the rose,
these blossoms of ideas and emotions I
have brought to the table to fashion into a work
that must not wholly betray them or ever depart
too far from nature as I perform this rite

that mimics but does not mock inspiration. I write,
diffident, slow. The impulse, when it arose,
both beckoned and taunted, and, now, knowing better, I
choose not to ignore what it might well impart—
a lesson in humility. That train
of thought, I have ridden before. But it could work

the other way. Against all odds, the work
might yet surprise me with some appealing strain
that charms. . . . But the sad truth is the spirit grows
weary and wary. My powers decline and depart:
I no longer can summon them as if by right
but, risking rejection, invite or invoke, as I

increasingly dislike doing. Or fake it as I
have done on occasion. For this did one study and train?
But imposture is also an art, and a person can write
better than he knows or deserves, and the work
may be more authentic, redeeming by these very throes
of composition the maker, who, for his part,

gives thanks to those gods he served but doubted. Apart
from that, what is there? The reader has every right
to ignore the entire transaction. Meanwhile, the work

proceeds and in rather better shape than I
can claim to be, for that bush it took years to train
now supports the trellis on which it grows.

Appearing upright still to the casual eye,
it is coming apart and will give way one day to the strain,
as mortality works its mischief upon the rose.

Foliage

The hillside, a dazzle of lemon, madder, and gold,
with notes here and there of topaz among the red,
or even vermilion, and copper puts on the old
display of trees in their wake for the year not dead

quite yet but dying. We've seen it all before,
but marvel still, driving along in Vermont—
or do for a while, but then it begins to bore
or, really, exhaust us with so much color we can't

take it in or respond any longer. The following week
is different: that gaudy party clothing is gone,
dropped to the ground, and instead we see the bleak
black trunks, the widow's weeds that they've put on.

But down in the valleys, a few trees still show patches
of color, indifferent to what has befallen all
their sisters, or else in a show of defiance that catches
the eye and the heart, too. And I recall

the story a friend told me of how, as a lad,
in the Radom ghetto, he'd confronted an SS man
after curfew, who'd reached for his gun but then had
smiled and, on a whim, let him live. There can

be such relentings, as these trees with their leaves
bright against the hillside's dun flank suggest,
such momentary fortuitous reprieves
beyond reason and for that reason blessed.

One could account for these trees still showing their bright
color, sheltered the way they are in the lee
of the hillside. Or we could see in the fading light
another more fanciful possibility,

that these bear witness to those millions who
are gone, as they testify in the chill air
in the ceremony that they continue to do
as long as they can, in patches here and there.

Death

An infant death can't move, can't speak. It yowls
and we're up all night with it during its colicky fits
waiting for it to exhaust itself and sleep.
It grows, or say matures, and learns to pronounce
a few broken words, then phrases and sentences: we
are proud of it as any fond parents would be.

Years pass; it learns manners. Then we notice
it keeps to itself, stays in its room, has its own
hobbies, or goes off to school, and we feel abandoned
and even fret, but then, for the holidays,
or for no reason at all, it will come to visit,
hug us, and even lift us up to show
its strength and the strength of its love, vivid as ever,
and assure us that it will always be our darling.

Soul

A body betrays, and even a mind can rebel,
but against what? What remains? Slowly but surely,
we are forced to suppose a soul, which serves us well,
while we serve it unfaithfully and impurely.
Infinitely regressive? Or merely shy?
Call it what watches, suffers, and remains
our subject/object, despite whatever pains
we may impose upon it, an inner I.

Or is it a mere fiction that one may admit
as useful or even necessary? Its truth
is theoretical, a series, a trend,
almost algebraic: and one conjures it
from the motes that fly in the thin air of his youth
to create the granite block that marks his end.

The Traitor Bird

From the Greek Anthology IX 551, by Antiphilus

Why does the town of Chalcedon hate
the heron so? Allow the great
Apollo to say: "On its spindle shanks
the bird that waded on sand banks
showed the enemy where to cross
to attack. O wicked bird! Their loss
they blame on you. For snails and kelp,
to betray your birthplace thus and help
those foreigners! We all disown you
and teach our boys and girls to stone you."

Colonial Graveyard

The rain has all but erased these gravestone names,
which we barely make out, or hazard guesses at,
as if we were trying to bring them back from the jumble
memory turns to. I look across to the Common

where Dawes set out with Revere on their famous ride
(famous, at least, for Revere). And Washington camped there.
Markers provide this information, but see
how letters, even chiseled in stone, grow weary

and yield at last to the indiscriminate raindrops
that mourn only the death of mourning. Relenting
is what these blank stone faces learn over time
and the promise they hold out, a modest gift
we learn in just a few years to value, the human
heart being smarter, or anyway softer than stone.

Birthday Poem

The stars shine with old light: what we see
has taken hundreds, thousands, hundreds of thousands
of years to get here. I rub my eyes and imagine,
looking into the past beyond my birthday,
what has persisted, as all energy does,
or so they say. The delicate instruments gather
astrophysicists' data, but can they detect
old sighs, old rage, old laughter that floats out there,

like music after the piece and before the applause,
cooling now and abstracted, but somehow still there,
as the Greeks supposed their heroes could be translated
into the heavens to shine forever? That giddy
feeling these distances prompt I recognize,
an old fear, soothed and crooned to by a humming
so soft I cannot be certain I am not dreaming.

Crazy Delmore

On my way to Harvard Square, on Ellery Street
I pass the house sometimes where Delmore lived
when he was teaching here.
                           We were almost related:
he was my first wife's mother's cousin Edith's
husband's cousin, and, on the strength of that,
forty years ago I invited him to lunch.
I admired his work and wanted to meet him, hoping
to learn . . . not how to write, but how to be
a writer, but what we talked about at the Yale Club
where I took him—showing off I'm afraid—was his hurt
and rage at having been, not long before,
committed to Bellevue for observation. (He'd thought
that Nelson Rockefeller was out to get him,
was broadcasting terrible messages into his brain
from the top of the Empire State Building; his friends
were probably right to have had him locked away.)
But he'd had, in the Bellevue psych ward, a heart attack,
and for quite a while the doctors there wouldn't believe
his complaints of chest pain. Now, what he wanted was justice,
and his liquid, slightly exophthalmic eyes
blazed with pain as he told me how various lawyers
had taken his money—he wanted to sue the doctors,
the hospital, city, state, the nation, and Nelson
Rockefeller—but then they'd done nothing, nothing.

I was sorry to hear how the lawyers were taking advantage
of a poor delusional poet and taking his money,
so I sent him to see my father, taking care to explain
that my father did not practice in New York City
but perhaps could refer him to competent, trustworthy people.
And my father, I said, wouldn't charge him.
                                          Delmore was grateful
and wrote on some scrap of paper my father's phone number.

It was, I realized later, a bad idea.
My father explained to Delmore how, while he'd been injured,

the law and justice are not the same thing, and courts
cannot right all wrongs. Any lawyer who took
a fee from him was a crook; and any lawyer
who took his case on contingency had to be crazy
or a fool. But this is not what Schwartz wanted,
not what he'd taken the train to White Plains to hear.
He started to yell at my father, who'd thrown out of his office
paying clients with better manners than this.
And Delmore Schwartz, too, he now ordered out.

I never saw him again, nor expected to.
A few years later he died, alone, in a cheap
hotel in the west Forties from yet another
heart attack. And this time he made the papers
because, for weeks, for months, no one claimed the body.

I told my mother it might be a good idea
for me to go down to the morgue and, on the strength
of our distant connection, ask if they'd give me the body.
I could have it skinned and stuffed and made into a hat-rack
for my father's outer office, and put up a sign
that this was the last man to raise his voice
to Sam Slavitt.
                My mother wasn't amused,
but now, whenever I pass that clapboard house
I see him looking ridiculous, looking angry,
his hand held out for people's hats, and his neck
sports the sign I told my mother about,
but the words have changed over the years, and it says
that there's no justice, that this is what can happen,
that writing is hard, but being a writer is harder,
that talent and dedication will do you no good,
are dangerous, even, and may, if you aren't lucky,
drive you to such despair and make you crazy.

On my way to the square, I often choose the route
that takes me past his house, so I can report,
chastened, how I have learned at last to read
the words of that hard lesson he had to teach.

from **Suits for the Dead**

(1961)

Warning

First, beyond all
song, or any note,
was that terrible small
silence in her lovely throat—
and all along,
the quiet potency for
most fantastic song.

Still, there lingers
in Philomela's cries
the echo of her deft fingers
when her music flies.
She could not sing
except for outraged muteness,
Procne, and the king

who had his wild will.
You, who would make bold,
beware when they keep still.
The tale is old:
quiet as snow,
a heart will burst—then warble
when the mind lets go.

Balloon

Even two years is plenty of downwardness,
the tiresomeness of it, the boring sameness of weight.
That the block with the zebra on it, splendidly flipped
with a speculative offhand sidearm more or less
toss, should not, even briefly, hesitate
but fall like a sedulous clerk, obedient, whipped

is an outrageous waste of perfectly good possibility.
Imagine, then, this too blue picture postcard
day, with the animals loping or sleeping in sun
and the air not cold but crisp with the civility
of good servants, walking from lions toward
okapis, gnus, giraffes, and coming upon

this not quite picturesque enough person with his
overpriced ice cream, his Cracker Jacks, and for the first
time in one's entire life, balloons that stand
up. Up! A haircut at Best's is
all one could want, but the balloons they had out are the worst
droopers and fallers and danglers from one's hand—

But these, most marvelously balanced on their strings,
these beautiful blue zoo hallucinations
of the crew-cut and, alas, un-Italianate vendor
sway with the wind: not mere imaginings
but real things of the real world on vacations
from its gross, gray gravity, or on a bender

with only a single strand left of sobriety
as though they were rid of their shoes, but encumbered by
the still recalcitrant laces. Familiar with jumping
on the big double bed, for example, and filled to satiety
with the creak of springs, the pillow's obesity,
the flatness of mattresses, bathos, the bore of clumping

back down, I bought one of the balloons,
green and giddy with gas, and brought it home
to watch it nose the ceiling like a goldfish,

only to see it lose that afternoon's
buoyancy, decline and fall, like Rome,
with that tired grace that is the final wish

of all extravagant high living. Back at the zoo,
having felt that sweet tug at my finger,
I should have let it go and lived its flying.
It would have been the humane thing to do.
But you ignore the elephants, don't you, and linger
to share the captive platypus's dying.

from **The Carnivore**
(1965)

Nursery Rhyme

for Joshua

bo
peep
little bo peep
little old bittle old o bo peep

old bo peep
little bo peep
little ittle bo pittle ittle o peep

o o peep
little old peep
bittle ittle odle ittle o bittle peep bo
odle ittle peep bo
little bo peep

hey diddle diddle and a little bo peep
little bo diddle hey little bo peep
fiddle faddle peep hey
bo bo peep hey
little diddle he pay
heap peep peep

bo
peep
little bo peep
had a little ho ho
goodbye peep

Ride the High Country

1

The long red underwear of Randolph Scott,
the gold-rimmed spectacles of Joel McCrea
underscore age, and through the reverend plot
the old gunfighters ride for one more day.

And Ladd was old in *Shane* and in *High Noon*
old Coop had all his wrinkles emphasized
(with visible distaste he drew his gun).
The ritual of honor is disguised

and is an act of memory and will.
The pistol-packing, popcorn-eating child
feels the pretended stubble on his chin
and imagines his bones weary after the kill.
Even the movies' West is no longer wild,
its *virtu* now a trail bum, a has-been.

2

Odysseus, safe at home, can be our friend.
Orestes and the Furies come to terms
—our terms: we, craven, crave the tamest end,
the fireside remembrances of storms,

the hero's diminution. The old hand
is slower on the draw, the eyes are gone.
We may admire, but we understand
that nerve is all McCrea is working on,

that aged manliness becomes absurd.
He makes mistakes out on the trail, he has
fallen into their obvious trap, is hit,
and crumples with gun blazing. On the hard
ground he shakes our comfort as he dies,
affirming the agelessness of what is fit.

F. A. O. Schwarz

. . . would needsly scorce,
A costly Jewell for a Hobby-Horse . . .

More than their children, they too are pretenders
whose tykes on trikes, their sons, they see sun-kings,
and bear them, like ambassadors, such baubles
as Fabergé designed and moneylenders
reckoned in years of taxes. And Schwarz's things
have still that high contempt of a million rubles.

Though crowns be gone, God save the attitude
of the dauphin playing with his cup and ball
as if to dare goddams to shake his throne.
On a four-hundred-dollar horse a diminutive dude
can look dispassionately on the fall
his France is threatened with, and wait for Joan.

"A Jewell for a Hobby-Horse"? The exchange
is better than fair. With the toy's extravagance
they mark the child as the last of royalty
who gallops, careless of their broadloom range,
and, sharing his noble disdain of circumstance
(his kingdom is a horse), swear loyalty.

Elegy for Walter Stone

*In August of 1959, I interviewed John Hall Wheelock at his home
in Easthampton, N.Y., on the occasion of the publication of* Poets
of Today VI, *which Mr. Wheelock edited and which included the
poetry of Messrs. Gene Baro, Donald Finkel, and Walter Stone.*

1

In the Apache over Hempstead with Finkel's view
of Fuji and the great wave in my hand . . .
But who would pretend to care? And why should Finkel
(not this particular Finkel, but any Finkel)
have a view of Fuji?
                              So I wondered whether
there was a first-rate delicatessen in all Japan.
An odd business this—when the mind takes off
leaving the body's ground, and the old terrain
with height is suddenly strange and unfamiliar,
when woods are smoothed to shrubbery, to lawn,
to plain green as the U.S. on a map,
when a Fuji is smoothed to paint, and paint to print,
and a craggy Finkel to an anonymous voice.
And the last is worst.
                              In London, on a grant
to study Renaissance eschatology,
the late professor and poet, Walter Stone,
committed suicide: an actual man
ground to a sheaf of poems that follow Finkel's
and in their total commitment to aesthetics
go his one better, for somewhere, still, in hiding,
in Queens, or perhaps the Bronx, surreptitious, Finkel
munches pastrami on rye (and afterwards
his tongue hunts for the caraway seeds in the teeth),
giving less of a damn for Fuji than, even, I.
Vive le Finkel! Which is exactly the point.

But let me be honest, for I too am a poet,
and the poet, Stone, is survived by a poet, his wife,
Ruth. And by Finkel (not my conceit, but the real

Donald Finkel, who lives and teaches at Bard),
and by his former students,

                              and by three daughters,
who ought to despise that rising, the lyric thrust
that can take a man up where he only guesses at Hempstead,
sees something important in a dead Japanese volcano,
writes—as Stone did—stanzas about a spider
so fine he forgets about his daughters and wife,
forgets even himself, and the piece of work
that a man is, speechless and on the earth.

2

Later: at night: remembering the plane
and the quick trip out to visit John Hall Wheelock.
We savored the horror of it on the porch
and then went in to lunch.
                              Hart Crane
I can understand. Jumping overboard
was, for him, the perfectly fitting gesture,
with all the grief of his failings as a man,
and still a passing insult to his readers
who cared for the wrong and expendable things.

                              But Stone
envied the angels' monotonous excellence,
their tuning-fork perfection, their effortlessness,
and even perhaps their wings . . .

                    The weights of the world
he shrugged off him, as if in a moment of pique:
his shoes, for example, in rows on some closet floor;
and his family, and his automobile, and his hairbrush;
and Vassar College itself, where the grass grows green
and the laundry washes two thousand bras a week.
The stupid stuff of the world . . .

                              He renounced it all,
or perhaps it was a kind of an embrace,
to become, after an unpleasant moment of choking
(or do you feel even that? Does the neck snap
like a pretzel stick and the life go out in an instant

without that terrible dwindling?), like a stone,
like a table, a part of that same dumb stuff
(with a frozen smile for the possible play on his name).
Not merely the notion of rest, but to be a part
of the created world, to rot, to change,
to become absolutely chemical, and godly:
this, perhaps, is more the poet's delusion,
fitting the paradoxical turn of the mind
which rejects itself by its own final thought.
Suddenly, there he was, as dead as a door,
and full of the same dignity as the door
in its wonderful knowledge of the real nature of substance.

Or did he wander off in that dark wood
to visit the *malebolges*, where they talk
in terza rima, suddenly convinced . . .
But no!
      Next I'll be calling out the dolphins
and making him into a hapless youth.
                        He died
taking his motive with him, and leaving us
to guess what his question was that had no answer,
and to think, with awe, of a man dead in his prime.

3

The plane banked to the left and suddenly landed
as gracefully as a sea bird on a rock,
and I stepped out into the forenoon sun
and the salt smell of the wind coming off the ocean,
and felt that slight irrational sense of relief
that the plane had made it all right, and I was standing
there, on the ground, waving to Mr. Wheelock,
who had a cab there, waiting. He told me how
he had once refused to go up in a plane with Lindbergh,
and smiled and remarked on the weather as we rode.
Nineteenth century outside and eighteenth in,
his house stands on a rise with a grove of trees
around it. Seventy summers it has been

standing there, where no other house is in view,
and seventy summers John Hall Wheelock has lived
through the rooms of his father's house and over the lawns.
But it is not virtue:
                             some of the good die young,
and some live long, and life is a random thing,
and the bus careens indifferently up on the sidewalk,
and the lightning, witless, streaks down into the park,
and the virus floats on the universal air.
It is not virtue, but a lucky chance
to which we attach perhaps too much importance
(and how we despise any quitting while you're ahead).
Wheelock was calm about it—regretful, but calm—
as we talked of Walter Stone, and then moved on
to talk of poetry or old pewter,
but there is no changing of subject at seventy-three,
and all the time he talked in one gentle tone
of the various guises of the one same thing
that a man must learn to gaze at, more and more:
Stone dead, and the poems left behind,
and the poems he would leave himself, and the pewter
and the house his father left, and the afternoon
perceptibly giving way.
                             Never mind how,
and never mind even when. All death is nature's,
whether by germ in the blood or idea in the head,
or sudden mischance in the wasteful order of things.
Gaze fixedly at it, and the distinctions
disappear.
             An unintellectual sadness
and a dumb calm is all I can summon up
for Walter Stone, for Wheelock, for myself,
for the act of imagination in Finkel's Fuji—
for all these sparks struck off by the turning world.

The Lemmings

Food short against the long days' hunger, sunset
a fatty morsel in the western broth, and sick
of racing the birds and the tides on the sandspit
for bits of edible sea wrack at which to pick,

it seems no more unreasonable one day
to try at last that sea that somewhere reaches
a western landfall, where each footfall may
fester with food, where it rolls down the beaches.

Thus their Columbus argues, convincing them,
for who has the strength to discuss or even care?
Slowly like a tide, they begin to swim
westward in the nobility of despair.

And if they never return, who can say the conclusion
is the obvious drowning it probably all comes to
who has stared for twenty minutes at the horizon
where the herring silver touches the herring blue?

Grenade Fishing

A pull of the pin, a lob, a plunk in the lake:
and then that moment of rippled silence before
the grenade goes off, and the lovely dead fish break
the surface, themselves, in pieces. On the shore,
a lip-smacking of water. For hook and line
and the sickening tug of the fish like a frightened insect
skittering down there, give me the anodyne
grenade blast, honorable, direct.

Angels ascending, the fish float to the surface,
loll on their sides, single eye to heaven,
while fisher rows and scoops with illegal net.
The oars plash with clarity of purpose
on the lake, metal-smooth once more. Morning's at seven
and the fastest is the best death you can get.

from **Day Sailing**
(1969)

Tableau à la Rousseau

That lions like lavender is amiable; for the mane's
tawny to find complement in the green
spike with the sharp accent of the blossom
is not mere whimsy, as delight in catnip
would be, but somehow right. One can nearly
see in those slow yellow eyes a need to express
the innate refinement lions have, and lavender
must be a relief from their usual provender
and the bloody obviousness of crimson with gold.
Or, it may be the odor, or
just to adore such a vegetable vegetable.
It extends the range of lions, even as they
extend its possibilities: they may
love most to patronize, to let it be said
that among the lovers of lavender are lions.

Sestina for the Last Week of March

Suddenly the ground is flesh and yielding
as if one walked on a body, and air is breath
and the woods are full of delicate, naked ladies
who hide in bushes and beckon behind the trees
in all the tempting attitudes of abandon
of the famous streets of certain infamous cities.

Who has not heard the erotic promise of cities,
or walked in squares with the light abruptly yielding
to shadows of unimaginable abandon?
But here, in the daylight and fresh air, the breath
of gin hangs on the juniper, and trees
carefully pose themselves like elegant ladies

considering some indiscretion. Ladies
learn to conceal such thoughts in civilized cities.
Oh, sometimes, in a formal park, the trees
will make their improper suggestions, conversation yielding
to difficult silences, the very drawing of breath
becoming absurdly physical: "Abandon

pretense, civilization, cities. Abandon
all the constraints by which you live as ladies.
Strip naked, lie in the grass, pick baby's-breath
bouquets, and flee for your lives, flee the cities . . . "
But they never do. That week of spring yielding
yields itself to summer. Leaves clothe the trees.

And yet, some must have gone. Behind the trees
those delicate creatures of our fancy's abandon
must have begun somewhere. There are myths yielding
many examples—reasonable ladies
of the kind one meets in fashionable cities
once, in the woods, struggled to catch their breath

and changed in the time it takes to draw a breath,
turning into, melting into trees.
Their stories are embroidered back in the cities,

tamed for us who can bear only so much abandon.
They have been refined, no doubt for the sake of the ladies
who know their truth and long for such a yielding

and for gentlemen of the cities, lest they abandon
fine careers, fine ladies, and run off, yielding
to the whispered breath of nymphs behind the trees.

from **Child's Play**

(1972)

Child's Play

Peter Pan flies in through the window.
They ooh and ah delight, surprise,
who do not see the piano wire
or the rigging in the flies.

They may suspect that Tinker Bell
is a light and bells (off, right),
but they suspend their disbelief . . .
How willful is delight.

Who is to tell them, then, that the fairies
are real enough? It's clear
that Captain Hook is a masturbator
and Peter, a raging queer.

"No one must ever touch me," he says,
not knowing why. But we know.
Wendy will be the lost boy's mother.
Peter's refusal to grow

is too specific. It's Masters and Johnson.
At the end of Act Four, it's corn:
"Do you believe in fairies?" They clap.
We smother discomfort with scorn.

But there it is, and true enough
to reach us, to make us squirm,
for if most of the little Peters will grow,
some will remain infirm

fearing the teeth of the crocodile's mouth
(the clock in the tummy? A womb!),
and sweating out Mrs. Darling's prayer
to the night-light left in the room.

Peter blows fairy dust on the children;
they fly, straight on till morning.
It's nineteen hundred and four again.
Vienna's a distant warning.

Their mother, nevertheless, is twitchy.
A face at the window? Who?
Who's there? It's gone. But it will be back.
It's me peering in. It's you.

And it's who we are, and it's what we know,
and it's what the children do not
(thank God) suspect about Peter, Sir James,
or us in this intricate plot.

Weeding: Florida, January

for A. Richard Pollock

Under an opulent sun, a *louis d'or*
or ormolu sunburst, riotous, rococo,
hanging like a lavaliere in the sky
over this last bastion of thriving
(have we not heard the news of Atlanta's snow,
the airlift to icebound Nantucket?) in bathing trunks,
I am weeding the patio, am rooting out
(*evil* you root out, *corruption, subversion*)
Bermuda grass, nut grass, sage, the grasping
weeds with greedy fingers that clutch topsoil,
reach down to marl and water . . .
                                    To hell with Darwin's
survival of fitness, the idea of the marketplace
of ideas. In this, my *orangerie*,
I will establish my own order, will promote
excellence, pursue grace, till my nails
are black with killing, pinching off opportunity,
maintaining inequality . . .
                            Like any king,
I know it cannot last, that eventually
the Bermuda grass will send its runners out,
set down its roots, choke out my delicate
favorites. Empires fall. We will grow old,
move out, take an apartment somewhere, and like Windsors
play jacks on a marble table at the Waldorf
or like that poor Swedish count, in après ski
kiss hands for dinners.
                        But not yet for a while.
And in the meantime, sweat pours down my chest.
The green corpses pile up. *Je maintiendrai.*

from **Vital Signs**

(1975)

Foreign Body

A foreign body will make the eyes tear,
will fester under the skin. We are xenophobes,
reject alien kidneys, hearts. Doctors
negotiate, their liberal black bags
full of blandishments, but the beast snarls
from inside its white cage a hatred of strangers.
We are separatists all, and our blood feuds
with other types. Children, innocent, die
from miscegenation of the factors. Bigots,
despots, each of us shrills from the balcony
me to the world's piazza. Still, there are truces,
treaties. Tourists learn *hello, goodbye,*
thank you, while dangerous men, polite, talk
careful nonsense at dinner tables and smile.
We are diplomats; we learn to be charming. The czar
wants to acquire a warm-water port . . .
I have my secret instructions, as you have yours.
But then, one night, we forget who we are, ignore
what we are. I accept, crave, cling,
as if to a dream of peace, to your foreign body.

Conquistador

A paradise Peru! That the cities are gold
hardly matters. We leave the home country
for adventure, carrying beads, knives, mirrors,
to barter for empires. The French, English, Dutch,
the Portuguese and the Spanish worked it. Why not?

I gave you cheap trinkets, scraps of my life,
movies, meals, sometimes a bottle of wine,
and like a jungle queen you gave sapphires,
rubies, a vast treasure, but knew what I was.
You knew the ship moored in our cove would sail.
I am no prince except by your grace and patent.

Ashamed, I think of my holdings at home. A pauper
would stay with you; a grandee could afford to.
The ocean should have been real; the true distance
ought to have hidden us. We pretend the jungles,
lagoons, and simple savannahs in which we play.

I can't stand it. I can't not stand it.
I take shallow breaths, one at a time.

Night Creatures

Imagine imagination that varies inversely
with being, so that elephants must lack it,
barely able to grasp their own bulk and weight
as they must be also deficient in deviousness,
thinking in straight lines from which they scarcely
waver, hacking trails of vectors with racket
they hardly notice, bulling toward a mate . . .
We must be cleverer, think more, being less,
who, to scamper from cover, must risk our lives,
touch only briefly, but dream and remember long,
like mice, like voles, those brave fools of the night
all men with mistresses become, whose wives
trumpet the truth: that we are small and wrong
and hopeless, and they are angry, huge, and right.

A Lament, for My Wife

Speech betrays. We have talked to one another,
promising, endlessly qualifying, refining . . .
What's unsaid is still true, that I shall desert you
sooner or later, and not just a late night
or weekend away—no such kind subterfuge—
but openly leave, for a cold, silent woman
with whom I am speechless, to whom I shall be faithful
as I have never been. What is there to say?
That I should stay with you, comfort, protect?
That I am behaving badly? My dear, I know,
but I have seen her in concert halls, in shops
where we have exchanged glances. I looked away,
but it was settled. I know that she will have me,
will take me into her irresistible arms.

Cruising

The weather changes, wind shifts,
tide turns, and too far
from the fixed line in all this heaving
blue-gray, I pitch into panic,
roll in regret for my carelessness. How
was I seduced by the glint of light
dancing on water, the pillow puffs
of cloud in the sky? Ride it out!
Bail, scramble, pray, promise
never to venture so far again,
ever to sail again, to sell
the damned boat . . .
                Later, alive,
land-legs back, and feeling better,
I am proud of myself for having survived,
and warmed with rum forget the prayers,
the extravagant promises. Try again,
when blue shall beckon and billow call
of sky and sea, or eye and bosom,
in bed or boat to reach and haul
from tricky winds pleasure and more?
Boats are made to sail in; men
are given to choose—to go down in them
or on the beach to die of dry rot.
The lines of a vessel can dance at rest,
tease to be tried, to move, Come,
haul anchor, love, haul ass.

Glass Exhibit: Old Sturbridge Village

A glass cane, elegant, fragile, useless—
a days-end whimsy from the molten glass
left after serious jugs, goblets, bowls
and from the breath left over and spirit left.
Paperweights, hand coolers, laundry pens
might, one suppose, exhaust the maker's impulse,
but down in the lungs there is always residual air
and back in the mind some static. So they worked,
played at work a few minutes more and made
glass trumpets, abstract series of joined bubbles,
all manner of physical babble, baubles,
extrusions from the lumps we are to intricate
creatures we might have been . . .
                              That atelier
produced flamingoes, platypuses, elk,
spider, squid, tortoise, mole, dugong,
elephant, and newt in the afternoon
when light and attention scattered to lush purples
that beckon at unreachable horizons.

Sooner or later, we will depart, but whimsy
keeps us at the bench a little longer,
to fool around, to make perhaps some trifle
worth taking along, or leaving behind.

Clam Digging

Haft rimed with salt, teeth bent
like an old salt's, its wire basket battered,
the clam rake lounges against the barn wall
as codgers will, and waits in the watery sun
for low tide and for me, dreaming of muck,
the Sunday morning grope in the old bed.
Rocks we get, old bolts, sea lettuce, mudders,
and sometimes quahogs. Throwing the rake out,
bracing it on my shoulder, bearing down,
hauling back, hip deep in cold water,
my feet in the ooze, I feel my toes go stone.
It's tough work, but I do little work,
have many toys, but only a few tools,
play at work. There would be honor in it
if I were hungry. The harbor's pleasure boats,
seaworthy though they be, make frivolous
flap of their halyards, cluck at the honest smacks
with old snow tires fishermen use as fenders
hung from their hulls. Are there natives and summer people
everywhere in the world? I heave and haul;
my shoulders and arms ache; I cut my hands
opening shellfish; my fountain pen will balk
in my bandaged fingers tomorrow. I do not belong.
Clams are excuses. I dig in the mud with a rake,
hunt for a natural self, look for a life.
The water, clear where I waded in, turns dark,
turns black. Minnows scud, shunning my stain.
I labor on, greedy to fill my bucket
with grace, with bounty, but willing to settle for clams.

Tough Characters

Ten things were created on the eve of the Sabbath in the twilight:
the mouth of the earth; the mouth of the well; the mouth of the ass;
the rainbow; the manna; the rod; the shamir-worm; the shape of
the written characters; the writing; and the tables . . .
—PIRKE ABOT, V. 9

You see them exercise; they march in fives
around the prison yard or work in the shops
at tasks we have assigned. We own their lives
or think we do until some mad one stops
short at the cellblock gate, turns, slashes,
and all of them join to riot. They can reduce
our institutions to meat, rubble, ashes.
You watch them always, and wear your sidearm loose.

They are not tame, will not do what we say.
Given the chance, they vandalize and kill
as they have always done. On the Sixth Day,
late, as if in afterthought to His will,
the Lord brought forth written characters: they
are savage, with the reek of Chaos still.

Le Babouinisme

We hung in trees once, and small boys will still
scramble up easy apples and eye the tall
oaks and elms. Our legend of the fall
goes back to that old grove we swarmed until
some tempting possibility on the plain
lured us down. With our opposing thumb,
we hefted a dead branch; we had become
hunters with clubs; but somewhere in the brain
a memory persists, lofty, leafy,
so that we, on a walk now, in a furtive hour,
look up to green sanctuaries, escape
our guilt for a while, and try to imagine beefy
baboons, gentle with vegetarian power,
secure in their grip on a joy we barely ape.

Intellectual Women

The negligent beauty of intellectual women
can turn a concert hall or a gallery
into a garden—those wisps of chestnut hair
loose at the neck arresting as some common
ferns, if they are properly placed, can be.
Not too precise. One wants that casual air.

They are always busy, making the good better,
their children, their communities, their minds,
and have no time for more than a lipstick and comb,
the good tweed skirt, and the gray cashmere sweater—
but you see the lines of the neck, the waist, the behind,
and know there's a body in which someone is at home.

from **Rounding the Horn**
(1978)

Poster

That it was cheap was not the only reason;
even for free, who needs a <u>Vogue</u> poster
of a lady in a long dress and a large hat
with a flowing veil, riding—sidesaddle, of course—
a rearing zebra?
                There must have been something, three
dollars' worth of message units, speaking
to our slight impulse. Do I believe in her
elegance that sits upon wildness, rides it,
and draws upon it? Is the farouche chic?
But, no, she would be smiling. Her face is clearly
wistful—and the zebra, rearing, is trying
to throw her off, run free, and join the three
giraffes in the middle distance. Her seat is sure,
though under the long green skirts we may imagine
the muscles of her slender thighs tensed,
feel them straining in the bizarre dressage
of animal and spirit. Those contradictory graces
are joined in equipoise: the zebra's strength,
the power of that striped haunch, that arched neck,
dissipates into her veil; and she is sorry,
knowing as the beast cannot, how long
their ride must be. She can never dismount,
can never be thrown . . .
                He could canter off
to fall to a hungry lioness, and she
could grow fat, perhaps, and old, no doubt, and gossip
at the watering places of fashion.
But, no, she knows
she is only a poster, the hot hide under her ass,
a Platonic idea of lust. An idea blows
her veil; a real wind coming off the mountains
would whip the damned hat off . . .
                If only it would!
Then something could happen—even something dreadful.
Which is to say, she doesn't believe in the zebra,
cannot imagine him, any more than he

has any idea what's up there on his back
but a body in a world of bodies, a beast
like him. He is certainly not impressed
by the silly beads about her neck, her shawl
of gauzy lime-green stuff. The bridle is real,
horsehide or cowhide, and the bit in his mouth
tastes of metal. He wants to spit it out.
His hoof marks scar the earth in dumb rage.
        Of course, they're together, then, innocent, gorgeous,
fighting to master each other and the picture,
and each needing the other. If the wind
were real it would come alive and end in an instant
to serve, stopped frame, as an image of earthly love.

In Poland, Pigs

Having roughly the body weight of humans,
the pig is a subject for tests of various kinds—
of drugs, for example, but also of man's (and woman's)
aspirations. All of us turn our minds

to heaven, hope for justice, pray that the swine
who cheated us, who checked us on this earth,
will suffer punishments, undergo such fine
tortures, we cannot imagine them; that our worth

will be recognized; that the meek will be blessed, the last
promoted first, and the mighty be brought low.
We wish, try to believe, and we hold fast
to such old and pleasant texts as promise so.

In Poland, pigs—or some of them—are dressed
in burlap suits, while others in the sty
wallow naked. Why should some be blessed,
tricked out in relative finery, and why

should others fare less well? The questioning pig,
assuming such a creature, would not understand
the obvious truth if he heard it. (One need not dig
for truth as sows do for truffles.) The grand

couture is perfectly practical. It protects
the pigs' skins, keeps them from getting scarred—
not for this pig's world, but for the next,
for the curriers' and the wallet makers' hard

scrutiny, and their customers', who demand
quality goods. The pigs know nothing of this
and do not pray. They do not understand
peace or justice, or try to imagine bliss.

The Vandal

With umbrella tip, spray paint, or even a chisel,
he visits upon museums his disasters,
whose name will never be listed among the masters'
nor even "of the school . . . " On the world's easel,

all he can sign is ruin. He must display,
the only way he knows, his life in art.
Restorers set to work. The damaged part
is hard to find as he is—carted away

to the proper bin, where in the day room
he talks not only of Michelangelo
but of Rembrandt and Picasso, "with whom, you know,
I have collaborated," and through whom

he imagines himself as he should have been, had one
of them painted his life. The subject was right,
but he botched it, splotched and hacked at it, in spite
of the masterwork he should have been and done.

True to his pain, and seeing the choice clear—
where there can't be credit—as one between nothing and blame,
he yielded to the urge. It's like a game
in which the guards defend, lest one appear

some afternoon to score for the disgrace
of having been wounded. We all learn thus to plead
with beauty: "Though I be ugly, though I bleed,
I love you; love me, or I'll smash your face."

Lobsters

When lobsters lose their shells, exchange
swollen discomfort for pain and a time
of vulnerability, do they
regret their loss or find some way
to enjoy themselves until the slime
that covers their bodies, tender, strange,

becomes familiar, hardens, grows
back as protective shell to hold
the world away? Or do they mourn
that the openness with which they were born
crusts? Young again, then old,
their gray-green cautions set, enclose,

and only delicate feelers remain
to question currents, poke the ooze,
and feel and feed through another year.
Human molting is also queer:
naked now, I hated to lose
the shell I shall hate to grow again.

Eczema

Tearing at my package like a child
eager for its present, I scratch my back
between the shoulder blades, my arms, my chest,
my face, and bloody myself, like one of those wild
self-flagellating enthusiasts. The attack
subsides eventually. Exhausted, I rest

but know another episode is waiting,
another battle in this civil war
my body wages with itself. My skin
erupts periodically; it's something hating
itself, the spirit revolting at the poor
flesh it must inhabit, is trapped within.

Doctors call it a psychogenic condition,
like asthma or colitis; it is an ill
in which the skin's itch is the soul's fret,
and scratching is the body's act of contrition.
I try to absolve with an antihistamine pill
and not to get excited, not to sweat,

but there is a rage inside me, a prophet's deep
revulsion at the flesh. When it gets bad,
I scratch as in a dream of purity,
of bare-boned whiteness, clean enough to keep
the soul that's mired there now, driving me mad,
desperate, righteous, clawing to be free.

Going West

Behind are those disasters of civilized
ambition which I flee, selfish and eager
for life in undemanding California
      where there are trivial

men and women who are all pleasant figments
of each other's imaginations—which is
what we'd all like the nerve to be, protected
      by miles, plains, mountains from

the distresses of our old imperatives,
ethical and cultural, the hurts of such
fussy Atlantic notions as honor or
      consequent self-esteem.

Here, where only a few cute missions are old,
where, in the sunshine of the present moment,
fugitives can thrive, flourish like lettuces,
      our faults and pretensions

diminished seemingly, for the only fault
worth the fretting about is that of the earth
we walk, not living and not building (those are
      proud words) but satisfied

to improvise for a while as in a country
where there are no cold seasons demanding thrift,
patience, the responsible postponement of
      all gratifications.

Winters and rocky soil with its promises
made for what we called stern character, taught us
to hold on, but here, no past, no future
      but a present like fruit

always in season lets us let go the tics
of Eastern time. I play with grown-up children,
frivolous, contemptibly happy as I
      hope myself to become.

Glaucus

What's the difference? All the gold in the world,
that solid eighteen-yard cube, isn't worth a thing
to a dead man. Lord Diomedes' bronze
could keep a spear point, sword edge, arrow head
from flesh and blood better than Glaucus' gold.
It's a better than even swap, friend. Take it!
Your life, and even your life with honor, for gold.
And Glaucus did, keeping his wits and head
on his shoulders to drive, alive, from the field into Troy.

My kind of man. But what's the difference? Later,
at the Greek wall, where not even great Lord Hector
could move against the rampart, Lord Sarpedon,
crazed with a holy hunger, a lion famished
for glory, hefts a pair of spears and speaks
to Glaucus, his cousin, his friend. And Glaucus listens:
    Biddledeegoo giddledeebah diddledeebee
    Honor giddledeeboo vines and fields
    Biddledeegah duty biddledeegee
    Wives children giddledeebah glory
    Deathless biddledeegoo we will attack!
So Sarpedon spake, the morning sun
kindling fire behind him, and on the wall
Menestheus, hearing it, scared shitless, hollered
for help, any help he could get—Tall Ajax,
Little Ajax, any Ajax, Teucros,
anybody, but quick . . .
                    but held the position
as long as he had to, waiting for help to come.
And they do come, the Telemonian Ajax
and Teucros, the bowman. Ajax kills Epicles,
smashing his brains with a rock, and Teucros shoots

Glaucus in the arm. He falls from the wall . . .

What's the difference? Sarpedon fights, and Hector
breaches the gate at last.
                            Gold, bronze,
honor, wives, country, giddledeeboo
biddledeegah, giddledeebee
                            Death
turns it all into nonsense, dulls the shine,
quiets the shouting.
                            He bought himself some time
(what else have we got?) worth all the bulls in the world.

Courtyard

A pennon of black nylon—I suppose
thrown from a window—a pair of pantyhose
drifted down to the courtyard and hangs there,
caught in a tree, embellishing the bare
branches. The wind plays with it, twists, furls,
and smoothes it. I have seen schoolgirls,
nervous, fiddle so with their scarves and preen,
discovering they are beautiful. The queen
of the courtyard, the tree appears to flirt with the breeze,
winds her fillet, and laughs with the other trees
that forbear to disapprove of how gaudily tricked
out she is, or complain that they were not picked . . .
Or so I hope, but questions run like cracks
in the plasterwork of these old buildings, the backs
of which overlook the courtyard: how and why
did pantyhose float down from the dirty sky
to snag on a branch? An argument, in which
some lover, absurd with rage, screamed out, "You bitch!"
and she threw what was at hand at him, and he
caught it and threw it out of the window, while she
felt more than that go, collapsed and cried,
while ghostly legs thrashed and kicked outside,
flying away as she would have liked to do . . .
Something like that must have happened. Nearly new
pantyhose don't grow on trees. The sprite
of a woman's nether half moved on the night
and grabbed at an opportunity, and still
clings to the tree. The wind's erratic will
arranges the hank of fabric, and rearranges,
making an emblem of the constant changes
by which the lower parts without the higher
writhe to the passing dictates of desire.
The North Hill quivers. I see, every day,
people carting their books and clothes away,
moving in and out in a slow dance
around the courtyard maypole that the chance
conjunction of wood and cloth has made the tree—

which makes it male. In its androgyny
we read what we can or have to, finding laws
in the rest and agitation of the gauze
the wind whips and the branch holds. No good
to worry about it, hope, fear what you would
or wouldn't do. At random, from out of the blue,
your token—a scarf, or pantyhose—falls, and you
look suddenly silly, gaudy, but sad,
and singled out. Your friends all say you're mad.
Birds avoid you. Nothing you do matters,
except to wait for time to rend to tatters
the cloth of passion, as always happens. The tree
will stand there, wait for wind and time to free
this tangle from it. All delight and grief
must pass. The furled bud springs into leaf,
dies, and is blown away. Sap falls and springs
up again and falls, but in the rings
of the tree's wooden heart, memories last
of flourishing seasons that hold an old tree fast
against new gales. What else is there to do?
Stand still, hold on, and hope to lumber through.

Walking the Dog

A dog will sniff at bushes, newel posts,
a familiar ivy bed, track his own scent,
and lift his leg wherever it seems right
to sign his claim. In pride of place he boasts,
"My territory!" And we pay our rent
and use the pot (until then, it's not quite
home). I walk the dog at night and think
of spots he's liked, his map of the good places.
He minds his cues and pees. "Good dog!" I praise,
uncomfortable. For us, *smell* turns to *stink;*
we are unhappy with our bodies' traces.
He does his business. I avert my gaze,
who can't return to my good places, shun
reminders that indict me, cannot say—
as I take him to be saying—"Life is fine!
I like it here." A cat, when she is done,
will cover it over and then go on her way,
fastidious, ashamed. Her way is mine.

Nudes

Gothic painters' scrawny
Eves and Adams shrank from
a Platonist Creator.
All Platonists are prudes.
Stripped of old religious
habits, we can bask in
the Renaissance's passion
for fleshly, pagan nudes.

The history of art yields
many such examples:
vision is a function
less of eye than mind.
Revolutionary
courage was required
before we learned to look on
beauty's bare behind.

But figurative painting
has fallen out of fashion.
The epidermal surfeit
of summer's seaside scenes
has driven to abstraction
those odalisques, who sulk now
on fold-out color pages
of certain magazines.

As distant grass grows greener,
so flesh is rounder, pinker,
hair softer, the lips fuller,
and the eyes a brighter blue
when beauty is forbidden,
glimpsed barely, or imagined,
and not the nude who's likely
to wake up next to you.

Still, we ought to offer
thanks for the suggestive

jostle. Greeks assumed that
the stranger in a crowd,
whose beauty was a kick in
the solar plexus, might be
Aphrodite, come down
from her Olympian cloud.

The Animal Act

Of course he knows what he's doing. The gun at his hip
is mostly for show, and when he cracks his whip,
it's to catch our flighty attention as much as that
of the graceful, silent, dangerous, lazy cat
perched on its little pedestal, blinking at him,
about to jump again through the hoops of his whim
and of our morality pageant in which rage
and lust may roar but lope back to their cage
every time to doze between shows. We know
its dreams of flesh, fear them, and would not go
into that ring for anything. Overhead,
an aerialist, blindfolded, plays our dread
for all it's worth, treading the high wire
above the lion's cage. Just so, desire
and fear in balance hold our feet on the straight
line of our intentions that keeps our weight
from gravity's jaws, or nature's. Or the beasts'
of the maximum circus for whom we are feasts.
Whatever roars or growls or screams in the pits
below the arena is eager to tear to bits
our delicate pretensions. The Romans' odds
were long but fair; they lived with what the gods
decreed, knowing that big cats are disaster
a few can fend off but no one can master.
In play, for fun, they maul, meaning no harm,
but a friendly swat of a paw can break your arm.
An affectionate lick of their rough tongues can take
your skin off. They sleep a lot but wake,
feel their animal spirits, and want to frisk
with their pals, their trainers, who accept the risk
as one of their rewards, knowing love's dangers.
We watch in the center ring an encounter of strangers,
of man and animal, in each other's spell,
and thrill, and worry, and pray they come out well.

from **Big Nose**
(1983)

Fairy Tale

And turned into a swan. The end, you thought,
because there weren't any more words on the page.
A warrant to suppose the uneventful
happily-ever-after? It's never that simple.
Yes, the swan was gorgeous, the kind of creature
you see once and dream of for years, a knockout—
the inelegant phrase nevertheless conveys
the sharp pain of perception there can be
at such beauty, that you and it can cross
paths. But after having spent all those years
believing she was a duckling and ugly, and having
been told by her classmates, teachers, and parents she'd never
do, she cannot believe herself in her own
transformation. Tell her the obvious truth
and all you get is a smile indulging your fondness
or else regret because it isn't so.
Some women were beautiful girls and know
their rights and powers as well as a majordomo,
setting out the familiar guests' place cards;
but the fairy princess, transformed, surprised by a wand
and set down at the ball is not at ease.
Your duty is quite clear. You owe it to her,
to chivalry and yourself to make her believe
the story you must tell her, her own story,
how, once upon a time, there was a duckling . . .

Big Nose

for Evan

1

The light bounced back a certain way from water
so that it sticks to surfaces as water,
and the trees all bent by the wind one way . . .
You recognize the set for your big scene
the lines for which you may not yet have learned
but the blocking is clear. You know you stand there, cross
to there, turn, and stand. The place speaks
as on a road at night for no reason,
a distant station caroms its long waves
off the ionosphere coming in clear,
CBC Toronto or Fort Wayne
for fifteen minutes as if it were fifteen miles,
the genius of that stretch of meadow, that stand
of piney woods. And you listen to it. Equipment
improves, seems for a while receptive. The place
speaks, and to you, looking like anywhere else,
but different altogether, the air different.
A dog would cock his head, or sniff, or dig.
Men and women, having lost those knacks,
feel uneasy, look uncomfortable.
A frivolous thought—if I were a millionaire,
I'd buy it, just to have, just on a whim,
maybe to mark it for coming back to, later.
Silly, but that's an example. The fainter promptings
frivolity allows us to attend to,
birds bet their lives and species on.

2

Two roads diverge . . . If they didn't there wouldn't be two roads
        but only the one, as any greenhorn kid
can plainly see. Correctly, it's one road that diverges
        to make the two—as at Salt Lake City, the northern
fork going up through Wyoming and down to Cheyenne, the other

running a little longer through Colorado
to Denver and up to where they meet again in Nebraska
near Ogallala. We took the shorter road
(I've no idea which of them has more traffic—out there,
it doesn't make a lot of difference). Rawlins
is on that northern road where 287 comes down
from the Rattlesnake Range, Muddy Gap, and Lamont.
We'd done our miles and were tired, entitled to sleep, and Rawlins
has a Best Western, a Holiday Inn, a Ramada . . .
The Ramada even has a Chinese restaurant
run by someone who must have screwed up badly
the last place he worked so that the tong sent him
here, close enough to the end of the line
to alert a reasonable man. It was the end once.
That singular, slender, singularly slender
brochure they gave us back in Evanston with a fill-up,
the entire cultural history of Wyoming
in its few pages, told us the story of how the railroad
ended in Rawlins once, till the line moved on
to make the next town the railhead. A brief boom
like what they'd had in Laramie and Cheyenne
came with the rail crews, the gamblers, whores, thieves,
and all that riffraff. Then they'd move on
and the town in a year or two would recuperate like a man
over a fever, a little weak in the knees,
but happy he could walk at all. That was the prospect
the sheriff of Rawlins faced and refused to accept,
considering it an affront to the town, the hills around it,
his own honor, and that of the clear blue skies
you can still look up at and damn near drown in, gasping at thinness
and purity and the clarity of stars.
I didn't see any deer, but grazing along 80,
antelope, and there aren't a lot of songs
you can drive out to check out and report back,
yessir, that's the way it is. Who knows
what quirk of arrogance or anal-compulsive behavior drove
the sheriff to do what he did? It beats me!
He rounded up a posse, the way they do in the movies,
Randolph Scott, and Gabby Hayes, and Yul

and Clint, and all the horses you can fit in a Panavision
        wide-angle lens, and took out after
the worst of the bad-ass boys, the crème de la crème, the pits.
        The last shall be first, it is written, and first of all
was Big Nose George Parrott, he of the epithet
        Homer might have found odd, but this is Wyoming,
where everything's got to be trucked expensively from the East
        so that anything home-grown, even a handle,
saves on horseflesh. Whether the malodorous reputation
        resulted entirely from Mr. Parrott's misdeeds
or was somewhat further wafted by the unforgettable name
        remains a question. My guess is the sheriff
braced a few of the barkeeps and the sons of habitués
        sober enough to talk. The pecking order
is clear enough in saloons—who gives way to whom.
        The point of it was exemplary, symbolic,
which gives our anonymous sheriff more than a touch of the poet
        or, anyway, ad man, which is a poet shrewder
than is good for him or us. The sons and daughters of Homer
        aren't all as blind as the old man was.
Big Nose George Parrott. In the sheriff's random sample,
        in all of his opinion polls, that name
kept coming up. Knowing that crime is rather like art,
        and neither ought to be voted on by those
who lack the proper training, that franchise not extended
        yet (or likely to be), he was nevertheless
forced to the rough pragmatic frontiersman's approach
        and, like a Bollingen Jury or Pulitzer Prize
Committee, bet on a name. They brought in Big Nose,
        tried him a little, found him guilty as hell
(of what, exactly, isn't remembered or written down
        in that brochure), and hanged him by the neck
—as judges say who dislike creative prison wardens
        trying to hang men by their ankles or nuts—
until dead. Yes. But they cut him down and then
        the sheriff came into his own, his scheme, his dream.
They flayed the poor bastard, peeled him like a potato,
        tanned the skin, and had the shoemaker (this
must have taken more than a little intimidation)

turn the hide into a pair of boots
the sheriff could put in his window, a shopkeeper's display
and warning. There was a little card to show
what the boots were, of what they had been made,
and to warn the world not to try to follow
in Big Nose George Parrott's footsteps or fill his shoes.

3

Some scenes, abruptly lush,
command us or, melodramatic,
stun like Yosemite, while others
we choose for our quirky private reasons.
Still others choose us:
that hollow where she stopped, turned,
assented, or a similar glade
unremarkable, innocent
today, but yesterday alive
with the whine of bullets and men's cries
in the soft green of the undergrowth
as out near the Wolf Trap festival
where it's hard imagining such discord,
or closer to hand at Gettysburg
where National Park Service Rangers
seem to intrude with their uniforms
on a place otherwise so pacific
and delicate, you'd think that grass
was all that could have been mown down here.
So, in Rawlins, the rolling land,
the clean air, the intermittent
riffs of traffic rolling on 80
and fading away to let the crickets
vamp for a while lulls the spirit.
One cannot imagine anything cruel
or barbarous spoiling a place like this
even though, on the road from Munich
to Salzburg, Berchtesgaden
nestles in hills that are much like these.
It isn't nature that cannot encompass

savagery, but we, ourselves,
having our limits. After a point,
endorphins take the sting away.
My cat once flayed a baby rabbit.
I couldn't believe it was still alive,
that red meat, a butcher-shop
window display, but still breathing.
I took the cat away and fetched
a shovel to smash the rabbit's skull
and put it out of its misery
(and, I confess, me out of mine).
I realize now, it was long since
past that line, feeling nothing,
a beneficiary of nature's
grudging mercy. Big Nose George
couldn't have felt the rest of it either,
after the drop and ejaculation
hanged men are supposed to have.
The rest was the sheriff's grisly doing,
not to him but the general public's
pity and terror or just disgust,
the manipulation of which he could
justify by pointing to
the prompt departure of maybe a dozen
troublemakers. Bad law
and bad art will turn official,
chew your ear off talking about
public safety and flashing their trick-
shop credentials: Junior G-Man,
Chicken Inspector, or Deputy Sheriff.
The set or the setting cannot save
the melodramatic historical farce,
even this. We left in the morning
and pushed on through to Omaha.
The skies were Hopkins-colored, the weather
threatened—a tornado watch
was in effect and all that day
a cloud's shadow followed the car.
Echo and Narcissus range

rough country where human voices
and human faces pop out of nowhere,
your own or one that's close enough
to what you recognize or fear,
speaking to you on serious subjects.
We've made Big Nose George a joke,
tamed as much as we could with gallows
humor, but it's two years now
that he's been tagging along behind us,
the shadow of a cloud or one
of those cloud-shaped Wyoming hills.

4

The great question remains: how does the spirit
inhere in matter, or how can the inert stuff
come to order, quicken, think? To deny
the spirit in things is as savage as to affirm
too easily how each rock, brook,
hill, or grove of trees entertains a god.
One must see the difficulty to see
the wonder of difficulty overcome
as on a summer night when the heat lightning
flickers in the sky and energy leaps
not in mere daubs of paint on a ceiling
but real, in the real world we stumble through,
or in the spring when the wind comes up and the trees
ruffle themselves and dance, like druids, like girls,
welcoming the rain. Wind and water
and light riddle us down to little children
and up to awe. Say lightning hits a tree,
you go to look, don't you, to examine
what is special, holy, a place where it happened,
an inspirited place where the silence of the hills
stretches thin so you'd think in another minute
something will give way and groan aloud,
or the river below break into sad song.
After the bums' understandable rush
to other less inhospitable places

the sheriff was left behind with those terrible shoes
and troubled and troubling looks from his friends and neighbors
to whom he had become a stranger, a marvel
like a charred, a blasted tree. Something had seized him,
some fury or demon held him and put him down
to walk their streets again. And it felt funny.
You don't just walk around in holy places
but take your hat off or put it on,
or your shoes, as in a mosque. . . . Those shoes disappeared
from the sheriff's window, having served his purpose
if not their own. People avoided his face,
looked down at the ground, their shoes, his shoes,
and more or less abruptly fled. He stood it
as long as he could, but weeks passed and months,
and people avoided him no less than before,
more openly if anything. He became
invisible and moved through the town like a ghost
in the company of a ghost. It wasn't fair—
what he'd done had only been for the town
(but not fair either). He stuck it out
a good while before he gave back his badge,
sold his place, packed up, and left one night,
those boots probably tucked away in the wagon
unless he'd tried to throw them away. Tried
and failed, that is, for they followed him. Big Nose
George followed along, up to Montana
and across the border into Saskatchewan
where he disappeared, looking for that holy
place to purge the holy taint he carried.
Spirit inheres, sure as hell, and tougher
to get out than dog urine stains
on your parlor carpet. And then the dog dies,
and you look at the place on the carpet and don't hate it,
treasure it, even. In Wyoming they tell the story,
print it up in a brochure and hand it out,
proud not so much of what happened in Rawlins
as they are that anything happened there and to them.
A twister touches down and it's terrible, brutal,
but afterwards people come to kick at the rubble,

sorry for the victims but awed and chastened
to stand at a holy place where earth and air
married to wake us from dreams of our poor devising
and remind us what they are and what we are.

Jacob

When I was a boy, I considered it boyish,
heartily gruff, nearly stupid—goyish—
for Jacob to have wrestled with that stranger.
The style of it was wrong, lacking the danger
of cutlass or six-gun and therefore petty,
unedifying, merely schoolboy-sweaty,
without the suggestiveness of hide-and-seek. . . .
Imagine little Marty Buber, weak
but wily, brow to a tree, his agile wit
considering whether he or God be It.
But wrestling? What on earth is a Jewish jock
doing near the ford of the Jabbock,
grappling, grunting, on the ground that way
with a sumo angel until break of day?
To that child's question, there is no reply;
the adult hardly thinks to wonder why
it could have puzzled, having spent long nights
in just such struggle and having learned those fights
are grubby, sweaty, and the muscles ache
from bruises only dirty fighters make.
Stiff in the morning, groggy from the bad
dreams that may have been wakeful thoughts I had
in the tangled night, I get up as sore
as if I had been held in a figure four
by some great goon—and think of Jacob who
struggled with guilt he should have been used to
from having cheated Esau whom again
he was to meet next morning. It was then,
you will recall, that famous match took place.
Coincidence? No, it was a classic case—
and the earliest reported, I expect—
of symbolic personification of affect.
But the label doesn't explain how, hour by hour,
the muscles tensed, the teeth ground, and the sour
sweat ran as he writhed in the tight embrace
of that thug angel breathing in his face
worthlessness and woe, regret, chagrin,

anomie, and the hopeless sense of sin
that lurks in all of us but works its worst
on the best of us. All night until the first
relenting in the east, he hung in there
in desperate struggle with his own despair
which knew and understood him at least as well
as he knew it. There was no fiend in hell
better informed about his wretched life
than this intimate stranger. Neither wife
had ever been so close, even in bed.
Its taunts all rang with truth. Discomfited,
he longed to yield: he felt his clumsy tongue
form the words in his mouth, but still he clung
a moment and then another moment longer
to silence and this stranger who was stronger
but with whom, for honor, he could still hold out
so many hard breaths more. And so the bout
continued—for the title, which he won.
Israel. Who strives with God. His son,
I can begin to guess what he went through,
take pride, and feel beholden as a Jew,
knowing that there's no help, that all alone
we wrestle with our angels on our own
at three in the morning. I have lain awake
uncertain whether my heart or dawn would break
first, and thought of Jacob, my forebear,
whose triumph doesn't help, although it's there,
a precedent, and has, I guess, its use.
The adversity of others can reduce
one's paranoia some. My father, his,
and so on back to Jacob, knowing how this
angel bullied, went down to the mat
bravely. What faith I have, I take from that.

To His Reader

Let us cut the crap. This old pretense
of a common decency or culture or even
sense is a dead horse the stupid cop
dragged around the corner from Kosciusko
to Green, which he could spell. Talk about stupid!
What else is there to talk about? The fine
modulation of a cadence? A pang
of remorse and a pain in the ass to the few of us still
able to pick it out. The rest don't
give a shit. Or shit all over it. You,
you son of a bitch! I'm talking to you. Listen.
You weren't my first choice but will have to do.
And don't try to wriggle out and join me,
turning tail, coat, and Quisling, leaving
them. Back! Down! What you lack in ardor
you make up by the smallness of your numbers.
Princes and counts, grandsons of thugs and thieves
were a fine lot compared to you whose agents
are department chairmen, lecture committee members,
editors, hired readers, losers, careerist
louts, toadies, turds. A pure indifference
is easier to take than this corrupt
inattentive attention you dare deign.
The expense of spirit is this—for years we are told
how virtue will be rewarded, but find out
it isn't true. Hard to swallow. Harder
is how virtue is punished everywhere
and always: any man who's not too good
for the job he's doing, isn't good enough.
That's pain, maybe not dramatic
(Help this child to live? Or turn the page?)
but fundamental, fraying the social fabric
at the seat of its pants. In a random universe,
that much order is tantalizing, taunting.
Who wouldn't retreat to his library, shrink
the horizon to a golden lamp-lit circle
of which he's sovereign? Exiled, diminished, bitter,

bickering as émigrés are always,
we form committees to write our angry letters,
learning to doubt each other until we are sure
of the grounds for our detestations. You are untrue
to all that made us special, worse than the hordes
of dummies we have always hated and feared,
having treated them badly (as they deserved).
But you, with your good manners, your pretensions
to civility and taste—you're a disgrace.
Junkies, hitting gas stations, go to pounds
for bitches in heat to occupy the attack dogs.
I used to worry about them, the addict-thieves'
whore-dogs. What could be lower than that?
An assistant professor of English, screwed from his job
by his department chairman the arts and sciences
dean has buggered again. Editors, agents,
reviewers, book buyers, the Dalton chain,
Waldenbooks, the seven paperback czars,
all your creatures, surrogates, your thugs
doing your dirty work, pretending to culture
exactly as you pretend, which is pretty badly.
Thief or dog, which should I hate? You squirm
in your seats and try to join me again, to agree . . .
By what right? You and Helen Vendler
deserve each other. You and Harvey Shapiro
invent each other every week—correctly.
The sovereign is still accountable for something—
the table legs and chairs that bear his name,
straight or curved, plain or carved, Louis
Quatorze, Quinze, Seize. . . . Demos, the one
and only, you are it, and responsible
for what you live with—this room and these chairs
first and maybe last of all. Grossfart,
King of the Visigoths, was finical
compared to you, chose which log to squat on
with a care and assurance you don't have. The poem
is dead. Its ghost is floating over the quad
when the moon's right. Its size and shape are the same,
but its weight is gone; it cannot carry the burden

it used to. You, the lovers of gravitas,
of empty ideas or fulsome descriptions of things—
furniture, fabrics, flatware, food, the dreary
novelist's flummery—you killed it. "I?"
says Turkey-lurkey. Right, turkey, you!
Its wraith, weightless, hovers where it walked,
trying to look the aristocrat gone some to seed,
but difficult to distinguish from the mad
unemployed who stare into crowds asking
why you and not me? resisting
the feeling of taint. It is no accident
but part of the art, its heart, to make us misfits,
self-conscious, as only impostors are,
and hostile. Like love, it's a disease
with predictable symptoms, a chronic debility
that may remit in the early to middle twenties
but can, in certain stubborn cases, persist,
intermittent, annoying, something like herpes,
trivially shameful. There is no cure,
but all of us are mortal. Medicine's failure,
inevitable, universal, and fair,
allows the consideration of other questions:
how to behave in the tumbrel, how to defy
the mob's garlicky breath, its mean delight
in cruel amusements, how to struggle against
the terrible temptation to surrender,
join them, play to them, and hope they'll admit,
after the blade has stilled their hubbub, awe
or some lesser acknowledgment . . . Who cares
what they think? Who even thinks they think?
Like God they tease us to believe in them,
popping up, just like those shabby sunsets
that blew the romantics away, or mountains, or sea,
the Theological Outdoor Advertising
Company's banal dioramas. Bullshit!
Dignity, however threadbare, turns
away from such displays. Honest is better—
to swallow the bitter spoonful (Good boy! Big boy!
All gone). I know you well enough,

as the mind knows the body. They need each other
despite their mutual treasons. Any idea,
noble or mean, mocks the flesh that bears
but cannot comprehend it. The mere meat
triumphs in the end. Even the glutton,
lecher, and sloth learn how it brings down
our temples of pretension. You and I
depend thus on one another and serve,
but you are not my friend. Nor am I yours.

Ramon Fernandez Recollects

for Robert Buttel

What he remembers is the portly Yankee,
down for a good time, walking the beach
to clear his head from the drink or to get drunk
just on the salt air the way they can,
and a girl singing. He got very excited,
yammering on and on about the sea,
her song, Christ knows what. He wasn't rowdy
but pointed at the fishing boats and the sky
and talked and then fell silent. It was his tie,
the way he never unbuttoned his collar button
or loosened his tie. That's what made him crazy—
not enough blood gets to the brain. In Hartford,
are they all like that? It must be very odd.
Still, he paid in cash and he tipped well.

Agamemnon Speaks

B 123–130

If we and they agreed, which is most unlikely,
but if. And we were then to divide ourselves
into groups of ten—to make the arithmetic easy.
Beside, eight is hard to seat. And six?
It's cheap; it looks cheap, the same way twelve
looks too formal, showy, and conversation
breaks up into groups. I've seen it happen.
So ten, then, and that's on our side. They,
and not all of them—only the householders—
come one at a time, as servants, footmen, or, say,
cupbearers, not that there's really a difference,
except that it sounds so primitive. Oriental!
As, technically, they are—oriental, I mean.
Anyway, if we wanted to do this, were willing
to go through with these strenuous arrangements
here, down on the beach, out in the sun,
or there, close to the walls, so that the cups
wouldn't have to be borne so far . . . I say,
at the right time of day, the walls' shadows
could make it fairly tolerable, the heat
being what it is here . . . It's a thought.
Under the walls then, the tens of us,
and for each ten Achaians, the one Trojan
servant. Well, you get my point? You see?

There really are more of us than there are of them.

Museum Piece

The signs are missing. Either one knows the names
of the streets or not. But the building numbers? Strangers
are not frequent here, *évidemment.*
Nevertheless, I find it, luck or instinct
having directed me right, the little museum
I've traveled so far to see. And, thank God, open.

The exhibits, also, lack labels, numbers,
are oddly arranged . . . A hand-printed placard asserts,
"The objects on view are only a small fraction
of larger holdings; each is specially rare,
old, or beautiful." But which are which?
Where are the guides or docents? Where are the guards?

Monsieur le directeur appears, abstracted,
but willing to answer a few questions. The guards?
An expensive pretension. Nobody comes to see;
why would they steal? The theme of the exhibit?
Significant Life Objects: A Retrospective.
Or *Instant Archeology.* Or *Junk.*

And the storerooms, he says, are full of it, and dark,
terrifying, and more than his job is worth
going down there again. The placard lies.
Still, having invested time and effort
getting here, I thank him and begin
browsing the curiosities on display,

unimpressive, pointless, until I catch on,
and then terrible—so that I feel naked.
Why is my life on display? That Indian hat
with colored feathers stuck in the corrugated
headband, wasn't it thrown away? The cases,
full of such trash, ridicule and indict

not only my unsuccess but my bad taste.
Magpies, packrats, are choosier. How could I live
with these things? The idea grows like a tumor

that my pretensions are not beyond question either:
if I preferred better, I had no right to.
These are what I was and am. This.

The conventional move here is to take it all
back, call it a dream, and let the sun
shine through a pane that is nevertheless cracked
and curtains that need washing. But love redeems—
or should—what habit can't quite blind me to,
and it's that love I invite or perhaps dare.

Last Days at Delphi

We used to speak for the god, with the god's voice,
and kings came to offer us their treasures
for our inspired treasure, while the breathless
world listened for what we'd say. No more.

We have become a tourist attraction, pretending
for small donations. . . . Oh, some old wives, provincial
and superstitious enough, still come,
believing a little. I think they are disappointed.
What can our hexameters mean to them?

The trouble is with ourselves no longer believing
(in spite of the world's indifference, the emperor's wrath).
Being illegal and going underground
can have—as the Christians ought to know—glamor.
I'd half hoped there might be a little revival
after Theodosius proscribed us.
It didn't help. One wonders why he bothered.

The Pythias speak, but only to one another.
Our white robes, our laurel leaves, our ablutions
in the fountain at Parnassus' foot, the stool,
the vapors from the cleft rock, the shivers . . .
We go through the forms, expecting nothing. The risk
is nothing. The emperor doesn't fear us.
But not to do these things would be rude, cruel,
would burden our burdened sisters with still more doubt.
Each of us has enough and has learned to bear it
each in her own way. Mine is to wonder
what other life I could make for myself, how else
to pass this month in the springtime, what possible use
to put this knack of making hexameter lines
as golden settings for paradoxical gems.

Besides, who can say, positively,
the god will not rouse? Apollo, nodding,
may yet wake, may wish to speak, to command
a new Croesus. How will the goats speak for him?

Nero plundered ten thousand talents here.
Shall I presume to rob Delphi of mine?

"Even if all of us here are frauds, I
am the best fraud." So each declares to herself.

Titanic

Who does not love the Titanic?
If they sold passage tomorrow for that same crossing,
who would not buy?

To go down . . . We all go down, mostly
alone. But with crowds of people, friends, servants,
well fed, with music, with lights! Ah!

And the world, shocked, mourns, as it ought to do
and almost never does. There will be the books and movies
to remind our grandchildren who we were
and how we died, and give them a good cry.

Not so bad, after all. The cold
water is anaesthetic and very quick.
The cries on all sides must be a comfort.

We all go: only a few first-class.

The Elm

       Late-leafing, as if shy,
it was pleased, nevertheless, to strike its best
       pose against the western sky;
but that last elm is diseased, my children tell me,
       and its branches die

       as if touched in June, in May,
by a bite of killing frost from an autumn still
       theoretical to summer people. They
can't understand it. I couldn't either, but
       having gone away,

       I've lost the feel of the year,
its times and seasons, jumbled them up, as that tree
       has, so that quince will appear
to bloom with the hawthorn, the burning bush, and all
       at once. It's queer

       how nature contrives to mock
one's frailties. So Adam, hearing word
       of the death of something he'd known in Eden—the roc,
dodo, or dinosaur—would feel . . . sadness?
       triumph? or shock?

       Not having the right to grief
or ground for any other coherent feeling,
       I can see each starving yellowed leaf
falling to leave a scar against the sunset,
       like a cross for a thief.

Ailanthus

The tree of heaven's a weed, grows like a weed,
its aspiration flimsy, its wood soft
for a wind of any strength to prune back hard.
In stands in vacant lots or along disused
tracks it flourishes, nourished on garbage, to rise
shameless where decent trees would rather die.
So the poor, believing, crouch in their churches
as if to spring, in towns we don't slow down for,
their hopes lofty, fragile, and nourished on nothing
but need for a heaven they can't even imagine.
Hardier trees, oak, maple, beech,
live where the breezes of this world may play
their canticles of praise in sturdier branches.
Richly rooted, such old growth is earned,
but even the dimmest rays of otherness rouse
this rabble with so little to lose to dream
their jumbled jungles in which cartoon beasts
scratch magnificent hides on their majestic
trunks, or glades where jellybean-colored birds
cry in their moonlit branches. Rubbish produces
just such rubbish in a refinement
of justice either exquisite or cruel:
we frame our prayers however we can, and angels,
delighted or dismayed, answer Amen.
That tree, because it stands on the line between
our yard and that of our neighbor, survives. No one
yanked the knee-high weed or chest-high sapling
or hacked the man-high stripling down (or could we
each have supposed the other might like the tree?).
By such dumb luck—our oversight, indifference,
and misunderstanding—it survives, thrives.
House-high now, it would cost serious money
to take down, with that phone line passing through it
to make the job trickier and more costly.
The Chinese were the ones who called it the tree
of heaven. Every morning in my study,
where my window overlooks it (and I try to),

it greets me with the day's first question: Why?
Such undeserved good fortune encourages all,
which ought to be heaven's purpose, to counterbalance
our lives here, refining this world's rough justice—
whether you stress the adjective or noun
(but that will depend upon your beliefs, condition,
and temperament). Your heaven and mine
will differ, but those malodorous little blossoms
must surprise us both who might have expected weeping
willows, say, angels could hang their harps on
sooner than this. There must be an explanation
homely and simple—perhaps that old soothsayers
and dowsers used the wood for divining rods:
or read the name the other way, as a warning—
an overgrown and overweening ailanthus
in the courtyard of one's house could bring bad luck
risking heaven's attention. That information
(true, by the way) answers but cannot exhaust
the nagging question—how the junk tree presides
over my lawn, vista, house, and life
to earn its name, teasing with possible meaning.
Poets have taught us how to look at trees,
how to stare at their elegant leaves for lessons
worth our lives. But this? It is slapdash—
which requires a child's directness, an adult's poise
to learn how to live with and how to admire.
A sumac gone to glory, the tree is a crude
patching of earth and sky on a boundary line,
demanding more than it offers. Heaven, yes.

from **The Walls of Thebes**

(1986)

Bloody Murder

Beauty and truth may dally together,
but when it comes time to pop the question,
it's ugliness that settles in
to take the vows with truth for the long
haul, the enduring and faithful companion.
The difficult lesson we all must study
is how to be children of such a marriage
and honor what we cannot love.

After the burglar bludgeoned my mother
to death with a bathroom scale and a large
bottle of Listerine, the police
recommended Ronny Reliable's
Cleaning Service—one of a growing
number of firms that make it their business
to clean up after messy murders,
suicides, and other disasters.

They have the solvents and strong stomachs
for such work. I still wonder
who would choose that kind of employment
or what the men who performed this awful
and intimate task looked like. We only
spoke on the phone; detectives let them
in; and the charge showed up on my next
Mastercard bill. But I know they were there.

The chemical smell hung in the air
of the empty house for nearly a month,
proving they'd been there and done the job,
which is to say that the other unthinkable
thing had happened first. Excess,
whether of pleasure or pain, beggars
belief so that lovers and mourners rub
their eyes in similar ways, trying
to take in the thought along with the image.

One needs both. On the KLH
radio my mother kept on
top of the bureau, there was a white
electric cord the assiduous workers
missed with its evidence a doubting
Thomas needs or dares, to challenge
nerve and love, the reliquary
stain of what had been done and undone.

It wasn't a bullion cube, would not
reconstitute in heat and water,
but there it was, to be faced, the mark
of faceless functionaries, furies,
or Ronny Reliable's Cleaning Service.
Jesus knew how it was—and wasn't—
a comfort to tell his stunned disciples:
this is my body, this is my blood.

The Whippets

At the levee, you remember all those busy
supernumeraries filling the stage
to represent not just the luxury
of the Marschallin's life but also the heavy demands
wealth can make on time and energy, problems
that burden only a few in the Grand Tier.
The milliner, chef, hairdressers in their mistress's
service command attention; other lesser
figures—the scholar, tenor, and noisy orphans—
beg and take what they can get. (The pushy
gossips, denied, will be back in the second act
to nudge the plot along.) Meanwhile, the crowd,
picturesque, dresses the stage and offers
the audience something to look at. See, in the back,
that vendor of animals. Sometimes he's given a caged
bird or maybe a monkey, or, on this occasion,
a couple of dogs for their touch of lively disorder
and also to balance the blocking. It makes for a nice
effect worth the minimal risk one runs
with animals on stage. Who doesn't have stories . . . ?
Of the horse in *Aida*—or was it *Fanciulla del West?*—
that heard applause for the tenor and, circus trained,
broke for the footlights to take its hard-learned bow.
Still, on a brace lead, a pair of whippets . . .
How can they fuck up?
                  The poor sod
stage director hadn't paid sufficient
attention to his libretto and its resigned
suggestion that our pretensions, or best intentions,
are doomed, even in love, or one might say
especially in love; and the pair of dogs
(as Frederica von Stade daintily put it)
"fell in love and got married," right there on stage
so that Dr. Bohm had to lay down his baton
and wait while the audience, on its feet, delighted,
cheered. Octavian stood there, appalled, although
the Marschallin was hardly disturbed and the Baron,

touched by such a display of innocence,
affected to stare out through an upstage window
at the prospect of a garden the sly designer
had indicated there, a paradise
to which the busy whippets were harking back.
They made a trio Hofmannsthal and Strauss
might have liked but wouldn't ever have dared
write, too knowing in stagecraft and too shrewd
in love to take such chances (how does one get
dogs that will perform every night on cue?):

OCTAVIAN

Is that what it all comes down to, rapture or even
faithlessness, that simple animal act?
They are looking at dogs but what they see is me
an hour or so ago. I cannot endure
the shame of having been found out, but she
queens it along as if she weren't still
damp with me there. However does she do it?
We are supposed to be sovereign over the beasts
but the truth is that beastliness masters us.
The heart and other organs lunge, slip
from the leash and run wild, or drag us along
helpless. Ochs is inured to it, thinks it's funny,
and she'd agree except that she's unwilling
to admit to such indelicate amusement,
which may offer a hint of how she'll think
of me in a year's time. Or will I be
like him, a lecher and cynic, remembering her,
if I do at all, as another name on my list?
It's true, dreadful and true, which is why they laugh
out in the dark pit, watching us fall
—or have we already fallen?—to their level.

THE MARSCHALLIN

That too, or that first and last,
but what we add transforms both it and us
to another realm, refined and elevated,

as the power of speech can turn a simple fear
or desire into articulated thought.
Civilization admits, or even depends,
on nature's crude *données* but, as at table,
we try to carry on with a little grace.
Tearing into their meat, would they offend
Octavian's tender sensibilities so?
And I wonder, is it on my account or his own
that he's distressed? Supposing the latter, Ochs
pretends to stare out of the window displaying
a delicacy I shouldn't find so surprising,
for I, too, maintain a certain posture
as in a *tableau vivant,* and feel the strain
increase with time. We must endure the applause
as if it were what we deserved for this *coup de theatre.*

THE BARON

Somewhere beyond shame, there's a shamelessness
for which we dig deep in the mud, a twin
of innocence. Those whippets, rutting away
onstage, are purer than music that hung in the air
like mathematics' body. We're old dogs,
my friends out there applauding and I, schoolchildren
again, staring out in the yard to study
the lesson a couple of strays taught, going at it
a dog's age ago. Where are those children?
What has time done to us? Or ask
how else to defy time except with that
repetitive stratagem? The joke is old
but still good for a smile if it's well told,
which is why they applaud. But see how the youngster blushes.
I would not change places, be young again
and run such risks—to be obliged to repeat
those strenuous exercises by which the soul
becomes at last limber even while the body
weakens and swells to what you see.
                                        They're done?
Yes, and the maestro raises his baton

for us to resume the pursuit of our quarry of meaning,
driven, perhaps hounded, but not forgetful
of who we are or where we are in the score.

≻☙

They settle down and return to the transaction
of the opera's business. Once again, the Baron
will pay and depart and, with somewhat better grace,
the Marschallin will exit, leaving the stage
to the young lovers, as she has to do in production
after production. The cast, timbres, tempi
and lighting vary some, but the action is always
exactly the same. Next time, darlings, the parrot
(one that never talks) or maybe the monkey
(but prepubescent, and wearing little trousers) . . .
Whatever "life" the scene may require we can
manage to indicate for intelligent people
who understand well enough the risks of love.

Tambourine

You think of gypsies, kindergarten brats,
and the glassy-eyed bimbo, always the least
adept of the group that calls itself musicians.
What does she do but bang it on her butt?

Pop and hiss, those contrarieties,
caught as they are in the tambourine's eternal
hoop, squabble, their bass and treble demands
upon our flagging attention, stupid, vulgar.

And music condescends to this, or aspires:
Baron Ochs, however else he is gross,
recoups a little, doesn't he, of our hearts,
baring his own with that simple wistful waltz,

its shallow depths his right and limpid pool?
What we remember of all the refinement, nuance,
and complication simplifies to that,
and the tambourine is the virtuoso player

of simplification flirting with boredom. Guess
if she or it be instrument for the other
to play—for we are not so circumscribed
as she. Acknowledge the little frisson they make

together, elemental, accommodating,
even promiscuous (any tune will do),
or close your eyes as hers are closed and conjure
any face you will. Dumb as she is

she knows how it is, how she's put upon,
but doesn't seem to mind as she dishes out
lucidities prefabricated for these
healthy inarticulate creatures, the forms

of feeling, the right vessels for what wine
their lives' *cuvée* may provide. The best will age,
mellow, deepen, but keep that scintillant
character, the nerves' tambourine thrill,

abstract, impersonal, and yet expressive
of what they are. Fortune, good or ill,
will compose the score, filling out the staves—
which is why gypsies, children in rhythm bands,

and adolescents, careering into the future,
like so well what most of us just suffer.
They bang and jangle, playing, thoughtless, eager,
happy, blindly happy. That's the skill.

Caution

There comes a time when you can bear no more,
some random scrap of news having proved to be
the straw that breaks your spirit's back. New York
has owls in every borough big enough
to take a good-sized cat? You feel their wings
beating the air over your head and resolve
    never to leave your house.

You recognize the rightness right away
of this avoidance of such pain and pity
as everywhere abound, but the sound of rubber
squealing on pavement, the silence, and then the smash
of glass and metal break into that tight circle
you've drawn. You draw it tighter, smaller, and promise
    never to go downstairs.

The feeling, nevertheless, persists of risk,
dreadful and universal. You don't quite trust
your mental status, but isn't that just another
proof, another worry? What can you do
but carry on somehow, as conquered countries
always have, and face it that you are likely
    never to leave your room?

With blankets drawn up to your neck, it should
be safe, but panic still takes your breath away.
Your heart races; you often break into the cold
sweats of the last judgment. The baseball bat
you keep within easy reach may be of some
use. There's no more retreat, now that you've sworn
    never to leave your bed.

Wilson's Pen

Wilson's Pen Is Ready. Thus, the headline announced,
the treaty not yet signed, their man in Versailles
still standing by. Some editor said, "Go!"
unaware that the banner's second
line ran the middle words too close
together and to the truth.

The second edition was different, even though
Wilson went ahead and signed with whatever
instrument came to hand—a fountain pen
no doubt, but Europe was no less fucked
for that. Self-determination
is a game history plays

rougher than gentlemen imagine and always
for keeps. But the newsboys' hoarse laugh, prophetic
enough, rings in the air every morning
still, for other reasons, as I sit
down at my desk to take once more
that unreliable pen

in hand in an attempt to perform the great trick
that may not, of course, work: so I risk chagrin,
by now an old companion. The odds are
always long. Even the big Mont Blanc's
burly power is null without
the consent of the goddess

to whom, when it comes, one learns to give thanks, knowing
how much is her free gift and how little skill's
desert. (Can women poets understand,
holding a mute pen, a mere machine,
what the ritual figures and how
a bared nib quickens or dies

according to the occasion, the concord of
cue and sensibility, not to speak of
how long it's been since the last time? Are they

able to fake this too, whatever
their reasons? That assurance we
sometimes envy but don't want.)

Our silences are what in the end give speech
its resonance, as the miles of barren sand
set an oasis, a jewel in that
dry shimmer. Would parched lips part to lie?
The pen, I say, has a will of its
own, will not be commanded,

and, as Wilson demonstrated, to pick it up
is to take our lives in our hands. The sword is
less mighty, even stuck into a stone
where it can say only *yes* or *no*.
This, though, can calibrate the soul,
measuring worth or its lack

with intimidating precision. It's said that
in primitive tribes, medicine men and chiefs
wear them, who cannot write a word. They know
magic wands when they see them and show
daring, as they would displaying
vipers asleep at their breasts.

The Last Dalmatian

1

Imagine, as I often do,
a woman, old and sick in her whitewashed
hovel overlooking the Adriatic.
The year is maybe 1902.
Once as a girl, she learned
words for *goat, fish, water, sky*
in her mother's mother-tongue,
what everyone in the village spoke—
but the village dwindled away, and the countryside
took up whatever Serb or Croat
dialect was then in use among
the townspeople. Dalmatian shrank to a joke,
the lyrics to songs, a proverb about the weather.
Curses and dirty words
survived a while longer.
But she was the last, this woman, really to speak
the language. No academician came
with tape recorder or even a notebook
to make a career by taking down
whatever she mumbled as she turned the air
briefly Dalmatian again,
losing each day a little more weight and spirit
until she was gone, her mouth a gaping
hole in the universe, or universal O
we all recognize as the mother-tongue
of pain and woe.

2

Each of us has suffered losses, each
has felt the terrible wrench of earth
shrinking beneath his feet.
There's less and less room to stand.
Gone are such exotic treasures
that once were the simple parts of speech.
What we mourn is not the body

but all those unmade sentences, rich
in history and desire, none
ever to be uttered now. The lexicon
and grammar have disappeared,
and Alexandria's library is burned.
If only I'd studied more and learned
by heart some of the basic texts. They're gone,
and I am the ignorant victim of my own
sloth. Grief and shame choke the random
smatterings I remember of English or Yiddish.
I am a parrot, can say, "Hello, hello,"
and utter at inappropriate moments a few other
simple phrases, telling all I know.

Wading

The tongue tip of the cold wave
licks your toes—it's great fun
to toy like this with so huge a beast,
apparently tame and lying supine
beneath a Crayola sun. You dare
a step farther and maybe another,
and feel the cold more at the ankles
and calves now than the feet, numb
already or somehow hardened to
the bracing water. You also notice
the weight of the waves as they come ashore
and their gentle tug receding. A dog
would tussle thus at a rawhide bone,
a puppy that hadn't any idea
of its size or strength, horsing around.
The sparkle, the salt, the bluish green
sluicing invites, taunts you to take
its challenge and a step farther
and deeper into the bright water,
and then the bottom falls abruptly
away just when you need it, when
a larger than average breaker gives you
a not so gentle cuff, and you fall
and feel the tug of the undertow
taking hold not quite in earnest
but giving you something to figure from
as you calculate its power and shudder
with a chill of fear as you clamber back
up the steep slope to the smooth
sand, a terry towel, and safety.

Months later and hundreds of miles
away from the moment, it still hangs
like a question mark, a wave about to
break and engulf the declarative
sense you thought your life was making.
The unpredictable currents—of passion,

disease, or fortune—that swirl harmless
about your ankles could at the next
innocent step bowl you over.

But you're no fool and have understood
that those are among the risks of the game.
Still, that feeling of being lifted
up and carried away by some
huge and indifferent power, that birds
and fish in the great currents of air
and water know in their fragile bones,
murmurs into the inner ear's
delicate balances, and you
go giddy, knocked one way by fear
and pulled back by the undertow's
embrace that waits like a patient lover.

Guts

All that fine-tuned high-toned discrimination,
where does it get you? Evaporating like foam
on the hard line of hot sand, it's cute
but has nothing to do with the depth or pressure of truth's

mucky bed. To feel in the guts is to claim
less but more, their crude fundamental reports
being of pain or not, distention or
relief, or the pleasant fullness of having dined

well. The head is a clever place but hardly
the domicile of the self, that big but shy
tube-within-a-tube, that deep-sea creature
of autonomic certainties you invoke

as too dumb to lie when something matters
enough for it to notice or care about.
Or let it be rather that lazy baby
you once were and still largely are,

with rage and content its only modes, brooking
no nonsense except its own. Words
always fail, don't they, and meaning, prior
and urgent, slithers away. That imperious being

is all you can trust—even when it comes
to the bad news. The five senses fool you,
but here is common sense, the sixth sense
you never like to speak of, even though

it keeps your manor going—or the chateau
where you play the lord while strains of music offer
genteel diversion; but you remain alert
to catch one of its slight but ominous rumbles.

Unveiling

Jeder Engel ist schrecklich.
—RILKE

Eddying winds, dust laden, busy themselves
in fitful domestic chores, polish
and tidy up, but over time grind down,
wearing the face of stone back to smoothness
as before the names got carved. Listen,
that sound the wind makes is that of the names
unsaying themselves in the grave mouths of the dead.
Among the living, too, gritty bits
of the world of matter that claims to matter
deface our clearest images. Details
relax their tenacious grip, run off
to hide in the barren landscape. Bereft
past grief to rage, we cannot think
how we could have let ourselves be cozened,
our losses so compounded. But it happens.
Vandals are merciless, and we share
in the blame, for those shy spirits
like all nocturnal creatures are easily startled,
and we are clumsy, noisy, and maladroit.
Worse, we prefer what is tidy and smooth.
Bad faith, bad taste, and fatigue conspire,
and pain saps our strength, even for this
impotent protest. Vulgar plaster saints
comfort, and the tintypes that grace our walls.
Forgivable lapses? Such violent forgetting
is no worse dishonor than what we do
throwing out old socks and underwear,
all those shoes, the ties no longer in fashion,
the vitamins and medicines, their cure
found at last. Harder to hold on to:
the imperfections on both sides, the impatience
on both sides, the thoughtlessness that marred
the tyrannous ideal we gave lip service
and to which we now promote them, doing them wrong

in a good cause, weeping, then dry-eyed
but no better able to see. The blindness
of young lust commends itself as charmed
and charming, or anyway necessary.
They settle on one another, persuading themselves
that he or she will do whatever it is
the script calls for as well as another.
Such indiscriminate longing turns
enemy in the end, its bad habits
of a lifetime the impediments and traducers
of love, which isn't clear and can't stand
still to look at what it claims to crave,
gaze fixedly at it, and then, eyes closed,
summon up the details of a face
worth all the world. The heads on Easter Island
are more expressive, better detailed. I forget
along with you, let go as I assume
that you are letting go: but then you pause,
turn back, reproachful, as vivid as ever.
Then, like Eurydice, you hesitate,
reconsider and disappear again.
These shocks, diminishing in intensity,
so exquisitely timed and calibrated,
welcome, precious, are not to be commanded.
For these ambiguous gifts, we learn to offer
our qualified thanks and admit that conventional prayers
for the spirit's repose are trickier than they seem,
pious impostures for—see—the eyes are open,
the cunning devil knows it's his own repose
he begs for, and at what cost:
that effortless glycerin tears should mark
the course that once his real tears tracked,
burning their way like lava. Fainter and fainter,
the artist pulls his engraving from the stone,
wearing the image smooth, as water or wind
will in time. The last loss is of loss,
the mind's failure, the heart's damnable health.

Old Photo

After years in a drawer with the film still in the camera,
its instants preserved in an Instamatic's belly,
it is not surprising that the prints come out skewed
to the rose we're taught to expect of memory, be
on guard against. The faces of my children
(when did Evan still wear those glasses, or Sarah
wear her hair that way?) help with the dating.
Mother looks the same. The Quinlans' tree
had not yet been cut down. Neither had Mother.
Josh clowns with a fallen branch from the oak
that still lords it over the yard. He thinks
that shirt was one he wore in the eighth grade.
If he's right, that was the last time all three
were there at the house together with Mother and Dad,
who never were much for cameras—which explains
how this half-shot roll of film got left for six
or seven years. I took it to be developed
to see what moment of passage, what special occasion
had prompted a last session of holding still
and smiling into the sun: the children's visit
on an ordinary summer day. The Purdys'
flowers are all in bloom in rose and mauve.
Mother's face in the one shot is far away.
Dad doesn't even appear. I close my eyes
to see better, but not better enough.

from **Equinox**
(1989)

Henry Taylor Shows Me His Parents' Barn

Beyond the condo's curtain wall, the Tetons
range, grand, wild, north to Grand
Teton and Teewinot—the brochures warn
of bears. I scan real estate ads, note
prices, imagine a life here, as all my life
I've done, on the Cape, in Miami, and other addresses
to which the rich and restless resort. I can't
afford more than to window-shop or to buy
a hat, boots, some souvenir to suggest
a recognizable past, but those hard faces
of gneisses and schists don't give. I'm not from here.
I think of the homelier hills in Loudoun County,
Virginia, where Henry Taylor showed me his parents'
barn less than a week ago. That country
is tame compared to this; even its shadows
must be familiar to one who grew up there; the patterns
of cloud crossing the sky are habitual; wind
that sings in the branches and brooks that purl in their gullies
are conformable to the ear as the songs one's mother
used to hum, unthinking. From the green
jumble on a boundary fence, he named
half a dozen vines, all childhood friends
of his and his father's, and further back. The barn
was one of a very few in that county that dated
back before the war, and he told me how:
his great-grandmother (I think it was)
took a chance—what was the risk if she failed?—
and had the barn emptied, all its provender
arrayed in the field he pointed to. The order
the Union detail had was to burn the barns
and the crops in the fields that Mosby's Raiders needed
to keep going. But the Taylor woman argued
with the sergeant or maybe second lieutenant that barns
were useless to Mosby; it was the *stuff* he wanted—
and there it all was. She waved her arm
in the gesture I saw her great-grandson enact.
Reluctant perhaps to seem mean to a woman

or impressed by her wit, by the sheer nerve of it, he
gave in, gave the order. And the barn
stands there still, not as old as the hills
but older than most of the barns in Loudoun County.
My grandchildren, my children, my sister and I,
our mother and father, their mothers and fathers . . .
none of us could put down, filling out forms,
the same place of birth two generations
running. Running, hating to look back, we
do not have maps on the walls with names of distant
uncles and nearby streams keeping each other
alive in memory. I envy and honor
that close connection to land, and fear for it too.
Washington's urban sprawl and Baltimore's
threaten. Less forgiving than that lieutenant,
invulnerable to shame and pity, they will
smudge his county's known features strange,
to the blur I drive through, fly over, land on,
and skitter away from, having no hill of my own,
no turn in the road, no color, smell, or light
like an old hat, conformed by usage to heads
I carry around in mine. I do not make
light of what it cost his people; it wasn't
easy, the barn standing empty, the yield
gone, like that, in a quarter hour's blaze.
It couldn't have been easy but it was
bearable—a small hardscrabble blessing.

Equinox

Ten Broken Stanzas for My Sister

1

A balance shifts, and we can feel the night
heavy in the scale; darkness and cold
will weigh with us from now on. In decline
the sun will make its doddering round of days
that are less than days, the ghosts of days; the weather
will turn; and the year, stricken, will sicken unto
death.

       It is all just as it ought to be.
This is the day when we call one another
to exchange whatever comfort we can. This is
the day Mother was murdered. And the sun
ought to blanch, to blench in shame. For all
our days are ghosts. This is our time of year.

2

In Yiddish, *Yahrzeit.* There is no English word
that serves correctly. *Anniversary*
is gay, wears party hats, has dinner out,
but *Yahrzeit* tells the time by throbs of pain,
mourns the turning of each season's screws
and can predict by inner aches the outer
weather,
            as the wounded learn to do
from predictable cycles of agony and numbness.
Pain and its diminution are the two
companions we trust, stars in our firmament.
We also have the telephone and each other.

3

The world being what it is, it has a term
describing us. The social scientists call
us "catastrophic orphans" and study us
along with survivors of floods and such disasters

and also torture victims. One theory holds
that the chemistry of the brain undergoes some change
so that everything else changes
                              for them, for us.
It's plausible perhaps. At least we know
that what we know, we know. The others are lucky
and, whatever their ages, innocent as children.
We talk sometimes as children, but hurt children.

4

One would suppose the past to be secure,
but no, its memories, even locked away,
are vulnerable to any passing thug
or crazy who can crawl through a cellar window
to wreak his retroactive havoc on any
treasure he fouls. The house, and the sense we had
of place that an alewife has or a spawning salmon
can find in its right river and freshwater pond
of welcome and safety is lost,
                              burgled, robbed.
Sickened, we swim through indifferent seas, all
salty, none worth notice. I would not,
hating that place, go back even to die.

5

Whatever people live for, happy times,
the milestones of graduations, weddings, births,
occasions of reunion and rejoicing,
these are tainted. Now, no good news comes
but with its confirming pang
                              that she has not
heard it, shared it, lived to see what she
would have blessed. And that lack of her blessing is
accursed. No child of ours achieves, enjoys
good fortune but to start our scalding tears.
Dutiful children, we rub our eyes with our fists
as she would have us do, we are sure, having
learned from her what good manners demand.

6

It doesn't get better. Years have gone by
and the only change is that we no longer expect
or fear that we may somehow regain our old
lives and selves. We are like the religious
brothers and sisters of some strict observance,
except that we do not pray, unless to bear
witness is a kind of prayer.
                              I doubt it.
What kind of play is it when Orestes
only shakes his head when Electra calls
to complain or, worse, not to complain but like
a good sister cheer him a little, to help him
bear it, bear up, get through another week?

7

The earth itself is the great mother, Gaea.
The Judeo-Christian view, always upward,
ignores such perceptions, primitive, basic,
as are under our very noses. The ground we walk
no longer springs, for the converse is also true,
that Mother was the earth. Her murder pollutes
like a chemical seepage or oil spill, and the fish
die and the birds and animals drop. On the news,
the clips are horrible, horrible.
                                    You and I,
stricken, can take grim satisfaction in these
dreadful confirmations that our worst
truth is not the exception, but that our
suffering has its company, is the rule.

8

We keep a few relics. I take care
of a pot of her African violets. Still alive,
they bloom in the spring and make me weep. But we,
being parts of her, are each other's keepsakes,
what's best of what is left of her, which changes
all the rules, for we must be good children,

tender with one another as if she had only
left the room a moment and would be back
to call us to account.
                        She is not watching,
which puts us on our honor. What's hard to learn
is to forgive each other, as she would have done,
and harder, hardest, to forgive ourselves.

9

All day I have been playing Pergolesi's
Stabat Mater, the melancholy of it
bearably remote: dog-Latin, Catholic.
And yet, the two voices, the boy soprano
and countertenor, are close enough,

                                    ours,
echoing, harmonizing and descanting,
as we do. *"Eja, Mater, fons amoris . . ."*
and I can scarcely breathe, for the gentleness
that cradled us from a brute and ugly world
is gone, and we are bereft. But like those two,
in harmony. A solo voice would be
intolerable. At least we are together.

10

The other blessing is that the cold will come.
The season is turning, has turned, and the first
frost will come with its usual relief,
killing by hundreds of millions flies, mosquitoes,
midges, and other such creatures that teemed and annoyed
for what seemed at the time a long time. The stars
will twinkle again in icy-clear air with a hint
of anaesthesia if not peace, those scary
spaces in between impressive . . .
                        We don't
believe in souls up there spinning around
forever like Laika but emptiness, cold,
and darkness are good enough. I'd call that heaven.

Solstice

A ghost of a sun flees from the sky as I,
the son of a ghostly father, hurry—to keep
blood circulating in the cold—to buy
another Yahrzeit candle in its cheap
glass I'll use for juice. I don't believe
in any of this, but he did, and I'd rather
feel like a fool than a bum. To think, to grieve,
to remember isn't enough. One must go to the bother
of doing something. Parents and children trade
places after awhile. I learned to endure
his whims and accommodate to demands he made,
as he had done for mine once. Fewer and fewer
remain except for this minimal annual task.
A postcard comes from the people who did the stone
that marks the grave, so I don't have to ask
what date the Hebrew lunacy falls on.
They put it to me: will I refuse to do
what I know he would have wanted? I give in,
go out, come back again, still wanting to
earn praise as the good boy I've never been.
And when the sun has given up, I give
lip service, mumble the prayer, and light the wick.
It's guaranteed that the little flame will live
the whole twenty-four hours, which seems a trick
for two and three-quarter ounces of paraffin.
All night shadows will dance on the ceiling and play
on the walls. And as I pass, I will glance in
to see how it's doing during the next day.
The flame is life, but the candle's guttering is
a reenacting of the death. I take
small satisfaction in my bearing this
as well as I do. I know it's for my sake
as much as his that I do this. My eyes brim,
but that can happen at the movies. Say
rather that I've bargained once more with him
and done what he wanted, only to keep him at bay.

Performance

This is like that. A modest claim
a child could make, and did, and admiring
faces beamed brighter than suns
at their son's promise. This is like
the fall: an amateur turning pro,
and the eyes rove, searching further
occasions for praise, acquiring dirty
habits of seeing and saying. Performance
and the hankering after applause distort
vision and skew the mind. The world
dislikes such preening; the smart-assed kid
gets sent to his room, rebuffed to sulk
and suffer. There, looking out of a window
he may find solace in how a branch
of the oak tree quivers after a squirrel
has made its leap—like the twitch of a nerve.
At it again? Now, however,
only for private comfort—another
compromise, another distraction
from the thing-in-itself. Even to glimpse it
requires reluctance, narrowed lids
and tight lips on which untruth's
unlovely taste lingers, a taint
one learns to loathe. Up in the sky
the only beaming now is from
a pale moon long ago
talked to death, but this is redeeming
recognizing that there's no
gain, no advantage; still he feels
sometimes an impulse, even the need,
irresistible, to break
a decent silence and admit
something even better, that rare,
clarifying, satisfying,
significant similitude.
It cannot beguile his old losses
away, but the small satisfaction

one takes in seeing and seeing through
is like a new stamp on the visa
pages of his limp passport,
his *permis de séjour* extended
at least for a while. A minor but vital
triumph, it perhaps deserves
a cognac with his evening coffee.

Canaletto's Ruin

Those clouds, stalled over what is left of the ruined
arch, are themselves another arch, their lines
a parallel that cannot be accidental.

Saplings growing, meanwhile, into the sky
from atop the masonry blur the hewn stone
to fluffiness. Canaletto's wit is at work,

as there in the human figures crossing the rickety
bridge or, below, in the boats on the dark water,
going about their business, diminutions

of the stone figures along the pavilion's roof
or of the heroic bust in the niche of the sunlit
wall, not yet abraded by time's roughness—

that shadow, nevertheless, almost too dramatic,
aslant at the base of the structure, is clear enough.
The day is nearly done, the sun about to

sizzle into the water—and yet the mood
is not melancholy, but rather, say, clear-eyed:
see the liveliness, there in the red tarboush

on the gondolier's head, or there in the loving
attention with which the wall's discoloring lichens
are executed. Such details redeem

or at least offer the comfort that nature's voracious
encroachments may be, for a while anyway, postponed.
This is, after all, a painting. The sun will not

ever set; the crumbling building will not
further dilapidate, nor will those human
figures progress even an inch in their

preoccupations. Ruin is what the painter
dares, defies, as he stretches his canvas taut
to assure us, even to catch us, panicky now

and almost ready to leap. That artifice cannot
last is what his painting says and then
unsays, which may be why we have an odd

vertiginous feeling, from contemplating a structure
not to be found on some backwater island
but in that shared dream (if not the nightmare)

Venice floats on like some improbable bubble
the lagoon has spat up that will at any instant
pop—and we wake to the realization of loss

of whatever we love most. That awesome wreck,
towering so as to dwarf the human figures,
is home, *signori, signore,* yours and mine,

if only we could steel ourselves to admit
so drastic a decline. Footfalls that echo
on those wide terrazzo floors sound in the mind

above the plash of oars—or are they whispers
of blood in the eardrum's artery? Those halls
from which we are overthrown are dark, filthy,

and repellent now, but we stare at them, fascinated,
clenching in impotent rage the useless fists
we never even raised to try to prevent

the disgrace we now inhabit, this abject ruin
we contrive one way or another to live with. Closing
the eyes should help, but doesn't at all—the image

persists. Those figures only maintain a civil
and mutual pretense, their glances averted
from the huge pile that dominates their lives,

and at night, alone, each of them sees his own
vision of ruin, as vivid as any painting.
Who then would need to look up, to confirm

his worst fears? They know perfectly well
what's there, can hear the water slap at the stone,
and feel in their hearts something like that stolid

coolness of stone that may be our best hope.

Fizz

Not altogether pleasant, as we remember
from our first sip, those little bubbles bitter
but also lively on the tongue, the tickle
a tart treat, but here was wetter water
to slake the thought of thirst. More popular, pop
cuts the tang with sugar, but this betrays
the charge of the thing, that almost metallic play
on the nerves of the lolling tongue's sybaritic meat
by the Vichy Celestin, Apollinaris,
Perrier, or simply Good Health Seltzer
in cheap litre bottles, that fluttery fizz
that, if it were any sharper, would make us laugh
or gasp. Even the best still water, chilled
and served in crystal, cannot satisfy this
acquired taste. On a hot day, the gods
came down from Olympus for ambrosia
that hissed and sparkled hymns as this does.
                                    So?

So . . . Let that crystal goblet with still water
be married love in its normative (natural?)
condition; and let the other be the other:
those lively bubbles are secrets, and the pressure
is the self-consciousness errant spouses learn
not only for what is obvious, self-protection,
but out of consideration—tact demands it,
and these are not unkindly people. The tart
truth that tingles so on the tongue burns,
hurts, but even for this one comes to acquire
a tolerance, even a taste, knowing full well
that if it were sharper, one would laugh or gasp.
Popular culture gets it wrong, puts sugar
into everything, but this alertness, charged,
has nothing to do with sweetness. Those who persist
discover what the gods on Olympus showed us
so often, coming down from their mountaintop
for the tonic of this ambrosia, this sparkle nothing
is quite like. This is that wetter water.

Satisfaction

News has come today that one
I hate and whom my parents hated
is stricken. His days are nearly done.
Would that they'd waited

to hear these tidings and to share,
as I think they might have, my reaction
which isn't pleasure so much as a bare-
boned satisfaction.

I like to think of how their prayers
and curses have at last an answer.
Patience is all in these affairs.
That he has cancer

and that all those nice metastases
are blooming like flowers everywhere
is charming news, but it would please
me more to hear

that his disease will run a course
both slow and painful—for my trust is
not in mercy but the force
of simple justice.

Let him writhe all night and feel
a taste on this earth of the pain
he's earned. If Dante's hell were real
and it could rain

molten lead down on his head
and I could see it and my father
with me . . . But he'll soon be dead.
Why should I bother

dreaming up elaborate
torments? What the world has served
up for him on his china plate
is well deserved

and will suffice. And when I rise
early to peer at songbirds flying
across the light, I'll rub my eyes . . .
and think, he's dying.

Lummox

As large as a water buffalo or larger,
but shaggy—there may be some woolly mammoth
in the bloodline—the lummox grazes the high plains.

Shy, easily spooked, they are homely beasts,
ungainly . . . Hell, most people think, plain ugly.

Every so often it blinks its large eyes.
Now and then, it yawns.

Hard to imagine, but thousands of years ago
they roamed the continent in vast numbers,
thundering herds of lummoxen, a moving
ocean of flesh, now storming and now still.

Is it fanciful to suppose some dim
dream persists of that stamping ground
to haunt the rare relict that now and then
startles ranchers or backwoods campers?

Nearly tame now and harmless,
its days of glory are gone, and we poke fun,
calling it clumsy and dumb.
It doesn't argue but only blinks, yawns,
then turns and ambles back into the woods.

Plodders

Consider the unclever. I
envy them rather. They do not try

but dimly rouse themselves to their half-
wakefulness. They never laugh,

say clever things, or write them. Stolid,
earnest, sober, very solid,

they go about their jobs and lives.
We are the ones who, sharp as knives,

have to worry lest we lose
our edges. They don't. Like old shoes,

they're comfy, good for years of service.
(We're unreliable and nervous.)

They are, on the whole, a happy crew.
I envy them. (I envy you.)

Circus Costumes

1

I never knew my grandfather, my father's
father. A figment, I had to invent him from
thin air or, harder, correct from the misleading
hints I'd got from the clinkers of love and rage
still warm in my father's heart's furnace.
Who approaches altars in the shrines
that families are without dread? Had he
lived, I might have seen him plain (grandchildren
can) without that shimmer of heated air
that rises so often between fathers and sons.

2

What do I know of my grandfather that I
trust, that I did not learn at secondhand
from my father? A picture, now lost, that I think
I remember; and my aunt's enlightenment
of why they moved to Bridgeport, why their plan
for a tailoring shop and gas station was not
totally crazy: the circus wintered there,
and my grandfather could make costumes for clowns,
acrobats, and bareback riders, silks
and satins, fancy suits with ruffs and spangles.

3

My father never mentioned this, preferred
the story of the atelier in Paris
where his father and uncle made the wedding dress
for Alexandra, a hundred women sewing
seed pearls on the train. Royalty! Class!
Or anyway not that louche other. . . . The low
life, like alcohol or other minor
vices, must not be made too much of. Let
the children have their first sips in comfort,
at home, or else it becomes a mystery, looms.

4

Or rather say there was too much love, a hugging
that nearly killed them as they clutched one another.
My father wasn't the eldest but the first
who was born on this side and lived. Another
brother came between Abe and him (Abe cannot
even remember the name), and my father was cherished,
spoiled rotten. With such delusions of grandeur
how could he admit to his father's life
and work frivolity, garishness, the glitz
of circuses, and their brown animal smells?

5

And on their side? What they demanded of him
I dare not even imagine: attainments, perfections,
the fulfillment of dreams no flesh and blood child
could ever manage. That he did as well as he did
was a marvel, but it cost him. To be ignored
I sometimes think is a great gift, as my aunt,
a mere girl, was—who later could afford
to take a job distributing skin-flicks
in which the performers kept their hats on and wore
(the studios must have been chilly) socks—costumes.

6

My father never spoke about this either,
although his sister's irregular regular wages
helped get him and his younger brother through school
and kept a roof over their heads. My aunt,
who thought it was funny, was right. And later she married
my uncle who traveled for Jewish charities with
those same curious films in the trunk of his car
to get the sports into a giving mood.
My grandfather, had he not been dead by then,
might have enjoyed the joke. But not my father.

7

Whatever they wore here, however they spoke
or carried on, my grandfather would have thought them
outlandish, clowns he kept in stitches. A man
with his griefs—that baby, that homeland,
the world's pretense at making sense gone,
ripped like a basted seam, melted like shoddy
goods in a rainstorm . . . What did he care what they
thought (whoever *they* were)? A man with a load
of heavy stones cannot imagine men
who bear no such burdens, who float, *Luftmenschen.*

8

On the other hand, drum rolls and the hushed attention
to those diminutive figures way up there
in Grandpa's flashy suits, bathing in light,
who dared thin air and leapt to their conclusions
on another trapeze . . . that was serious stuff,
death-defying! Would the clothing, discarded,
be soaked in blood or just sweat? Is there
a difference? My father didn't think so. Exams
at school were trials, as, later, his trials in courtrooms
were exams, high-wire acts in the family circus.

9

It is spring; the sap is rising; and the rubes
rise to their feet as we climb, rung by rung,
that awesome pole that holds the big top up
to the tiny platform. Down below, your father
my son, stands watch as we whirl over his head
like gnats, like furies but tiny at that distance.
We would call down assurances of our loves,
but he can't hear us, fears for us, fears us,
as we let go, fly off, fly back, and hug,
holding onto each other, as if for dear life,

10

but nowhere near so desperate or serious. Later,
from our dressing room, while getting out of our costumes,
we hear the drums and applause in antiphonal salvos
but give our attention to hangers that stir in the closet
like wind chimes in a garden. As if in a séance
it could be Grandpa signaling his approval,
or merely a greeting. I have his name; we have
his blood; you have my grandfatherly love—tepid,
comfortably vague, and yet reliable, like
an old socialist's dream of brotherhood.

Used Furniture

They lug elderly sofas and tables in
and out, chests, credenzas, rocking chairs,
and nightstands into their stores and out again.

When the weather is fine, they leave some on display,
out on the sidewalk. You go to the liquor store
on Market Street and you can't miss them, poised

where the slums and student housing meet, which is right
and how those stores have lasted. Nearly worthless,
the pieces of furniture move with a life of their own,

survivors of deaths, evictions, and even sometimes—
as when a number hits—good luck. They find
a comfortable level of hardship to hang out with,

shrug off, or give in to. In their glare
we try not to let our apprehension show:
in that part of town it is provocation, even

invitation. Spirit's the thing, booze,
bought by the half gallon. Safe at home,
I'm jumpy but keep my feelings hidden. The lesson

still holds, for I know where some of these tables
have stood and the chairs have sat. Where will they go
from here? Don't ask! In the heart of the wood, stirring

as if in a breeze that once tousled boughs
of the living trees, predators' screams and their victims'
cries are barely stilled. A chair, a table

will turn on you, will suddenly turn vicious,
or, like some bitch in heat, take off one day
to mill with her own kind out there on the sidewalk,

comparing scars and daring the lives to come.

from **Eight Longer Poems**
(1990)

The Wound

1

The spear is his alone. Nobody else
can heft its ash shaft. His friend, Patroklos,
borrows the rest—and loses all but the spear.

His father's, it is his, his heritage,
a mortal weapon, a mortal's weapon. The gods
had nothing to do with this. The shield, the greaves,

all those layers of corselet and girdle
Hephaistos made, they make a pretty story.
But Achilles dies. It is his nature to die.

His actions, therefore, are serious, as the gods'
can never be who float on forever, their feet
not quite touching the dark earth, their blood

a colorless ichor. Death is the long shadow
Achilles casts. And Peleus' spear, his father's
ash-and-bronze weapon, is properly his,

as Thetis has to learn. It is hard for her not to
avert her eyes from the corner where it looms,
propped with his armor, its omen all too clearly

shining in sunlight and glinting in firelight.
As much as his heel is his, his spear is his,
stands for him, and means him like his name.

2

Those old men must have known
what they were saying, what they hinted:

to those who could understand, it was all
clear as water; to anyone else,

dark as water when wind blows
to ripple the surface slate and silver.

For Telephus' wound, the only cure
was a touch of the same spear that made it,

Achilles' spear. Poetic justice?
Yes, and perhaps lore from the old

healing arts from the age when spears
were pointed with iron—the rust would have been

curative in a wound. Still,
the specification of that spear,

Achilles' own—what were they saying?
A part of the plot, to make the killer

also the healer? A homeopathic
remedy demonstrating the double-

nature of people and even of things?
Troy cannot fall unless a son

of Herakles help the Achaian host!
So had the Oracle warned them all,

and what other son of the hero is here?
No way around it then, unless

Achilles help his enemy, touch him,
heal with the spear that is his alone,

and therefore share between them a bond
they both feel, and the same shame.

3

Or
was the
spear nothing
in itself, but
an implement for
the production of pain?
Was it, perhaps, the same pain
in which the cure's magic
lay concealed like a
whole tree in an
acorn? The
balm was
tears!

4

We have all felt the liquid fire, burning and annealing,
the hot rush of our tears that are the anodyne
for the pain we feel. And any tears will produce
at least for a moment that wonderful ease, the release
of the spirit's suffering. Tragedy does it, the pity
and terror will turn the faucets on and perhaps prompt us
to remember our own lives' disasters, our unassuageable losses.
But a day later or only an hour, and we are no better, no
different from what we were before the start of the evening's
entertainment.
        But suppose for a moment those tears
you were shedding were not just any tears, not Lear's
or Antigone's or Aida's or even Bambi's mother's,
but yours, the identical tears, provoked by the very same
pain that had first produced them. . . . The old scars
are not so insensitive. They seem tough but they are only
hard on the surface; underneath there is a dull ache
that will not go away, that you have known so long
as to confuse it with the normal human condition,
or anyway yours, your nature being always to feel
that not-quite-disabling throb or twinge or frisson.
And then at that same occasion, the same production
of tears that turn out to be the right and only solvent
for that odd amber or exotic epoxy that had frozen
the disabling hurt into its place in the heart's
heart, the soul's most secret chambers.
        The talking cure
of Dr. Freud? What else is it but a reaching back
to the source of the pain, the source of the original
tears, or to speak in myths and parables, the touch
for Telephus of that spear? Achilles' spear
made the wound in the first place, goring his flesh
and tearing from him those tears; only a new
outpouring of those same tears will make him whole.

5

The issue of Herakles' rape of the princess Auge,
he was exposed newborn on the mountainside. . . .
But we are, let's admit, all of us, children of lust
of which we are ashamed and afraid, and we were all
exposed newborn.

What else is it to come into this world? And the long
odds of our being saved by the mercies of a goat
(or was it a shepherd, or, in Pausanias' version,
an open boat tossed by the waves?) . . . The chances
are never good,

and we are right to feel rage as we blame those huge
monsters upon whom we depended for their betrayal,
even knowing how helpless they were, how they struggled
with forces greater than themselves—mountains or waves
that dwarfed them down

to a helplessness almost as abject as ours. We cannot
afford such generous understanding that tends to loosen
our grip on the single issue of life and death,
our own survival. Telephus is wounded
as each of us is

in the deepest part of his being, his infant's love
for his mother—who of course turns up again,
in Mysia, where he arrives after many years
of vicissitude and adventure, to rout the foe
(Idas the Argonaut,

but it hardly matters; there's always a foe and occasion
for battle) and he is rewarded, offered a bride,
the king's adopted daughter, and the rite is performed,
but just as they're ready to consummate their union
a horrendous serpent

comes slithering in between them, for which thank heaven!
because you and I have figured it out already,
our ears pricking up at that "adopted" business.

Auge, of course, is his mother. He is saved yet again,
but that doesn't help,

because sometimes the thought is as good or bad as the deed.
And who has not had such thoughts? However deep
we bury them out of the light, they come in the nighttime
to worry our dreams, to suppurate, and ooze
their poison like wounds

that won't heal. Which is why the almost incoherent legend,
not having been built up or reduced by some major
dramatist, persists, as a buzzing in the ear.
The certainty is that we have been hurt and deeply,
which is why we hope

for a cure, no matter how strange or from however unlikely
a source, even as strange as the rage of Achilles
which is our own rage, the mania—we'd all assume
if only we had the heroic or brute strength
to impose our will

and exact the satisfactions to which we are
entitled. Lacking that, we must supplicate
the power, plead what has harmed us be turned to our use
for justice's sake, or pity's, and kiss the rod.
Let the spear heal.

Monster Dance

1

To address, to engage a small child, you must be
a child or admit that child who hides in you
in a drowse, rouse him, and let him get up and play,
tucked in as he is for grown-ups' time, the games
you never quite forgot. Another language,
you used to babble in it. Rusty now,
its idioms come back, and you take flight
as birds can with maps in their tiny brains.
This is discourse other children respond to,
will even let go of a mother's leg for, trusting
at least a little; you can't help feel flattered.

2

My son excuses himself as he might do
for an unavoidable phone call. Just for a few
minutes, he says, to do his Monster Dance.
In bed upstairs, his son waits for whatever
my son is going to do, does every night.
The huge shadow he casts from the baseboard night-light
wars with whatever menaces in the corner
shadows to scare my grandson or lurks behind
the bulk of his bureau, in depths of his closet, or under
the bed he lies on that used to be my bed
and ought to be safe but isn't. It never was.

3

A child has nightmares. What has he to fear,
cosseted so and cuddled, who's never heard
a harsh word and lives in a Peaceable Kingdom,
its plush animals ranging his walls? Griefs
that await, he cannot imagine except as cartoon
wolves or ogres who fee-fie-foe but never eat
anyone we know. Fum. My son,
foolish with love, is making a fool of himself

prancing about up there, an amateur shaman,
to jolly his boy, startle him into peals
of laughter that work nearly as well as magic.

4

The magus descends, rejoins us, and we eat.
No one refers to the rite stuff. Hours later,
when I go to bed, I think of the child, that younger
self on the other side of a plaster wall,
and the wars of fear and laughter, of good and wicked
darknesses he wages. A car goes by,
its beams of light sweeping both our ceilings,
to keep the monsters cowered in closet corners
he thinks they hide in. I know it's worse: they're slyer
and burrow inside our heads, camouflaged in the vulpine
rages and lusts Sophocles braved, and Freud,
to prey upon helpless lambs, defenseless kids.

5

Can I remember my son my grandson's age?
Time tumbles us headlong. Fear of falling
that newborn infants are thought to begin with, I
still feel in the night stillness. Floors
give way, and I stare into yawning abysses, gaping
like mouths of beasts time cannot tame (they gobble
even time). The only defense there is
is drastic: to learn the heaviness of stone,
of the dull black boulders that human hearts
tend toward. We hit bottom and sit there,
secure, or that's what we think, but a trivial movement
disturbs the scree and begins an avalanche.

6

Fighting panic, I baby myself with a wish list:
imagine my son inviting me in to watch
or join him in his grands jetés. We'll leap
together: the monsters will flee, will not come back
for weeks, and my grandson will sprawl in my bed,

snugger than boulders. They must dream of floating
weightless in blue sky, even as raindrops,
runneling down their flanks, find hidden weakness,
infiltrate seams, and freeze—which is how a stone
cracks open and, eons later, its dust
will ride the winds its improbable dream foretold.

7

My son is faking. He knows that, I know,
but my grandson has no idea, believes in monsters
but trusts in his father's Monster Dance. When he's
grown, he may perform it with more assurance
for his children, with someone else to blame
for the stompings and wavings of hands, the darts and feints
he'll barely remember. Shadows battle shadows,
but the sweat is real and the blood, while the furniture
shimmers to insubstantial ghostliness.
Houses dissolve; coastlines shimmer and dance;
but gestures one took for granted endure like granite.

8

They sleep: the nervous three-year-old is nestled
cozy in his belief in his parent's love;
across the hall, his father no longer needs
such demonstrations, which I'd find hard to provide.
Fearless, as he should be at the height of his powers,
he dreams only of what he wants. Awake,
I am the fearful one, but there's no help
from a distant heaven, other and better than here.
This stillness is hardly prayerful but like an extruded
instant in which, after the squealing of tires,
one waits to hear the impact of metal and glass.

9

Exhausted, I fall at last into restless sleep—
another arena in which I'm tormented by
hostile creatures, nearly human or super-
human. I flee; I run as fast as I can

but barely move. I would cry out for help
but my voice is gone. Impotent, infant, helpless
(those to whom I looked for help are gone),
I know that this is a dream and dawn will break
with a pallid light that will change nothing. I'll dress
and, not to frighten the children, smile and say
that I slept well, performing as well as I can
this variation upon a familiar step.

History of My Ear

for Brendan Galvin

1

I sported badges of bloody campaigns such as no
implausible generalissimo ever would wear.
My recruit's first pip, hidden away, was almost
forgotten—but that's another story. Parades,
when peace breaks out, degenerate to charades,
and the martial music turns tinny. Bystanders
jeer and call out advice on where to stick it—
in your ear, of course. Hamlet's father ought
to have taken better care, to have given or lent
ear to that buzzing at one of the seven gates.

2

To turn a deaf ear, you have to have one.
With my good side on the pillow, I could sleep
like a baby, but then I was a baby. My nights
are rougher now—the racket comes from inside.
There's nothing to hope for. The quiet I have already
tasted will soon enough extend itself,
as if I had lain all those years on that narrow
patch where the backhoe will come to chuff
and scoop the sod for me, that good ear
to the ground like an Indian's, listening for hoofbeats.

3

Ingmar Bergman says that there are only
two kinds of films: the documentary . . . (And?
Musicals?) Almost! "Dreams" is what he calls them,
whether a hundred showgirls tap-dance on white
pianos or the business is rather grimmer.
The right was my documentary ear; my left
was what was left, the way for another music
to conceive itself in intervals between
louder events. The better the fountain pen
the smoother its nib, and the closer to perfect silence.

4

Children daydream, romp in recesses, hide
and seek, as they play, trying on and out
those dreams of life that may come true, dog them,
come to heel, or snap at their heels. But later
such respites turn on them and spite them. The hard
lessons the hard of hearing learn is retreat
from attention to conversation. One gives up
and sinks into that shred of baby-blanket
silence he has never wholly abandoned,
by now a ratty rag, black as a shroud.

5

The Oticon devices have nothing to do
with the scourge, but we worry, nevertheless, that these
aids intrude the world upon us, so it
becomes, as a retrovirus does, us,
or what was encoded as us but is now that ruin
a self would resist if any self were left.
The mute key on the TV control is a clumsy
substitute: one forgets, and commercials blare
while the virgin nerve the broken drum protected
thrills to be learning the other's whorish tricks.

6

The center shifts. The sensation in the normal
ear, which is used to doing all the work,
is of deprivation. To share is to be deprived.
The dumb brain in its box tries to work it out—
if the sounds are equal, it must mean they are loud
but something is wrong with the right ear, and I yawn,
knowing better, to clear the Eustachian tube
that isn't clogged. They say it will take time.

7

Tiresias may be patron of blindness, but who
speaks to the deaf (or shouts at the hard of hearing)?

Evelyn Waugh, who affected an old ear trumpet
until some bright young Mayfair mayfly poured
most of her martini into it . . . ? Nasty!
They made them with sherry then. Beethoven, surely,
whose music, after he loses his hearing, becomes
increasingly cerebral. From deep wellsprings
it oozes up, thick and black, from levels
of silence only bad ears ever fathom.

8

It teaches patience, attention, and how to read
the meaning of moving lips, or on those faces
where the lips are set, the mood the eyes betray.
Inward, that concentration reaches to treasures
monsters guard. A poet's ear can hear
what dead voices whisper, nursery jingles
and lullabies a part of him still intones,
observant as any monk. To take these vows
is only a start; he then must wait for the world
to hush, fall to its knees, and join in prayer.

9

That it doesn't breaks his heart, even though he knew
from the start how absurd an idea it was. What child,
having done well, will not look up to the beaming
sun of his parents' praise in which to bask?
He is not proud of himself but of the rare
gift he was given, and from which he has given
everything. That nobody cares is the last
hard lesson it takes almost as long
to master as the craft. Another silence,
he greets it as he would a familiar, a friend.

10

What sounds do the stars make, or our cells,
dreaming themselves into being and burning fires
that rage or gutter and die? That there can be
poems changes the stillness. Think of a phone

that at any moment could ring, that waits to ring
in a silence therefore different, leaning into
the future. In such moments of eerie quiet,
as between a lightning bolt and thunderclap,
one learns to live. The air tingles, the whole
body strains to hear . . . I am all ears.

from **Crossroads**

(1994)

Ida

Sweet as apple cider, yes,
but rather dowdy, like a loose housedress
with flowers on it, Ida, she decided,
wasn't her, and she would not abide it.
Many girls reach more or less the same
conclusion and reject the name
their parents happened to give them; only a few
persist in this notion and conjure out of the air
something better. Fred and Adele Astaire
were dancing together then, and they had chic
and style, as much as anyone the week
my mother went job-hunting and had to choose
something to put on the form. Few Brooklyn Jews
were named Adele, but even Brooklyn was
a part of America, with bright promises.
Adele danced into her mind, and it would suit,
she thought, as well as any. Not too cute,
but not too plain, not Ida.
                              Years go by,
she marries, has two children. My sister and I
grow up. At length our father dies, and she
is killed, and only then, when it falls to me
to order her grave marker, do I learn what
her real name was, from her elder sister. But
not real: her friends, her children never knew
Ida was what she once had answered to.
Adele, she chose herself. Therefore, I put
that on the order for workmen to cut
into the stone.
                              And if it is not she?
Then she has eluded the angel, wriggled free,
and is that girl again, out of harm's reach
as when she left Manhattan Beach
that ordinary morning. The subway came,
and on her way to Manhattan, she picked a name.
Whimsical but also brave,
such spirit is not contained within a grave

or troubled by the wearing down
of arbitrary characters on stone.
We are spared too, who have no cause
to blame ourselves for any memory loss
of what we never knew: she remains with us,
inviolate, and nearly anonymous.

Crossroads

for Vera

A lowering sky, a wide expanse of stubble
in empty fields, and two roads crossing where
the village houses, leaning together, huddle
    against cold Polish air.

I see that dour landscape clearly, although
I've never been there. It could be from a story
we tell to children—but then, on second thought, no.
    Why should we have them worry

as we do? Nothing remains of that crossroads
hamlet. One street, I'm told, had the better houses;
the other was where we lived, of course, but those
    gaps close as the time passes.

It was for our sake our grandparents gave it up
and left the place, things, people they belonged to
for the dream of somewhere safer. On the trip
    that thought was what they clung to

for dear life, and, alive, I'm glad they came,
but what they abandoned is what I dream of now,
asleep, while people who don't even know my name
    monitor consoles that show

what zones in my house have been violated—what doors
or windows opened, or motion sensors tripped
by the cat or some intruder. On the street, cars
    are stolen and stripped

by desperate men, wild children . . . Who can say?
It isn't safe here, or anywhere, and God,
stunned, still mourns at that crossroads, far away,
    where also the dream died

of the Socialists. (The Zionists' went later.)
Over those empty fields, the wind's low moan
keens for those who died there together better
than we die here alone.

The Penitent Peters

for Paul Weiss

1

There are two St. Peters—El Greco's is on the right.
In a dazzle of light, a heavenly scrutiny, he
prays for himself and for all the world, suggested
in schematic boughs overhead, a human figure—
possibly female—off to the left, and way
down the road, a sketchy town, backlit
in the sunset. Lean, aristocratic, gnarled
(look at those arms!) he intercedes for us,
and there the keys to the kingdom hang from his belt.

But across the double doorway of the Phillips
Gallery's music room hangs another Peter,
Goya's, who also prays. And there's no world,
but only a brown background, admittedly paint
of which he, too, is part and parcel. His
is another kind of prayer, and he is another
kind of man, a saint but plump. Low forehead.
A man of the poor people . . . One could say more.
That he once might have been a Simon, could have been Jewish,
Yiddish, even id-ish. Emblematic keys
are nearby: he has put them down on a rock,
setting aside for a moment a weighty burden.
He prays, I assume, for himself: O Lord, I am not
worthy. But which of us is? And who will take up
on our behalf the heft of those ponderous keys?

2

It wasn't to gain the world that we put our souls
at risk—but only to know that the world is there.
Our body's boundaries bound us, closed us in.
Beyond was mother, was other, and we were othered,
orphaned, as often enraged as enraptured: we sickened
with longing. Goya's Peter, at ease, at home

in his painted world, is already closer to heaven
than anything we can, in bereavement, dream.
He hardly requires those keys he has at hand.

As he prays for the world, he faces the doorway. Across,
in the line of his vision, El Greco's Peter ignores him,
the eyes raised to the source of a blaze of amazing
light. Those representations around him that we
notice, he disregards, having quite taken leave
of all that men have learned to cherish, placate,
and appease—the world's body, which may not be ours,
but reaches toward us as mothers do for children
sick, even to dying. (Aren't we all?)
But he no longer takes notice, has already turned
his eyes away and upward to pray for the world,
for us, as he prays for himself, oppressed by the weight
of that light of God in a heaven where there is no
other, and where, at last, we may be healed,
whole, and—though we cannot remember it—home.

Lullaby

The words are worn down to the bare
tune's bones, but the song sounds
in my head in my mother's voice, thin
as if it had carried by some trick
of air over enormous distance.
In the sharp shard remaining, a bird
appears, I assume having flown for miles,
to sit on the singer's foot. It bears
a message, a love letter she thinks.
After a bit of business (the bird
cocks its head, hops, or perhaps
bows) the singer reads the note
the terrible tenor of which we may
have hazarded guesses about already,
given the minor mode of the music.
Her longed-for lover is dead, but the singer
is able to take some solace from
the ridiculous robin or wren (it was not
one of the nasty pigeons my mother
despised). Before departing, the bird
sings a song, and the song stays,
a kind of consolation—absurd,
or so I supposed, but I was a boy
and could not conceive of such a loss
or imagine how people in pain will grasp
in their free fall at anything solid,
some sense impression they can turn to
in trying times of senselessness.
Now I know, and the bird flutters
and sings in my mother's fluty voice
that song I remember her singing her baby
fighting fatigue, reluctant to sleep
and let the world for which he was greedy
go. The bird obeys his script
and takes his perch on the tip of a toe,
lively as ever. The lover is dead,
and the music mourns his loss. The tame

but heartless bird delivers his message
chirping into indifferent air
in which his darker cousins caw
their sterner dirges for which my mother
may have been trying to make me ready,
for the night sky is no nursery
ceiling: its pale and pitiless eye
is not that of a patient parent
watching over her stubborn son
and crooning as he fights against sleep.

Poems Written on Hotel Stationery

1 Las Brisas

A cliff . . . they often put these hotels on cliffs.
Birds dart across the sky making squeaky-toy
cries of delight. (Or are they hungry?) Below,
we see the sea and can descend for lunch
in the shelter of thatch. Outside, in the sun on the sand,
natives trudge, hawk silver bracelets, dresses,
hats, kites . . . One girl sold toy rats.
We repair up the hill where the greatest demand upon us
is the daily death of hibiscus blossoms they put
in the pool each morning to drift and waterlog,
and lack of stress is the only stress. Each day,
we inspect the sunset. Later, we'll have a nightcap
under the stars and over the constellations
of lights below, the town we look down on that clings
to the hem of the mountain's skirts across the bay,
and wonder perhaps what they can dream of down there.
It is up to us to see what those dead eyes
cannot imagine. They take for granted the hot
sand that has burnt their soles to the toughness of shoes.

2 The Inn at Spanish Bay

From across the dunes at sunset, a piper skirls:
the simple meeting and merging of fire and water
as the sun drips from the raspberry mille-feuille
confection the sky has become into the silver
foil of the ocean's wrapper is not enough,
so management tries to retain the patrons' attention
by such bizarre grace notes. And the motif is
Scottish, after all. From the golf links: Troon;
St. Andrews; why not a piper? Nevertheless,
the kitchen is northern Italian, some higher-up
having drawn the line, thank God, at haggis. It works,
one must confess, and that nature, naked, requires
tinkering. No place, no event is ever
sufficient unto itself. At Pebble Beach,

tee shirts allude to Maui, as there, to here.
To sit still, to be wholly where we are
and be content even with luxury, sunsets'
spectacular shows of the sky and the sea, demands
too much, is too expensive, exclusive. Heaven!
It's almost all one could want. But it costs the earth.

Sentence

The bread was stale, her father explained—no good.
Sixteen months old, she considered this,
processed the information, and then announced,
"Eat bread, duck-ducks," referring to mallards
that scrounge on the pond in the college garden they visit—
my daughter, son-in-law, and she, my daughter's
daughter. A rather Latinate trick, to hold
in suspense her emphatic subject, but she will learn
handier ways to modulate and stress.
Still, her meaning was clear and clearly beyond
the first business of pointing, of sticking labels
to objects: baba (bottle); bow-bow (dog);
or baby. Better and better articulating,
clarifying like cloudy tap water that stands,
there were nouns first and, later, modifiers:
"Elena's book," or simply a "blue hat."
But this is something new and utterly other,
with subject, verb, and object dancing now
behind her glittering eyes. It is not the wrath
of Achilles, or man's first disobedience and
the fruit of that forbidden tree, not yet,
but it's what she needs in order for them to happen.
Call it the plain the citadel looks out on,
or the empty sea beyond at which they stared,
shielding their eyes for their first glimpse of a mighty
armada rumor had said was on its way.

Tatiana, Older

The innocent passion she has lost hangs on
taking us in, who recall our own and mourn
that such transports are gone. Onegin, remember,
was not even there. That he was clearly queer
was beside the point as she went on and on,
enjoying her suffering even more than we,
for loving is always better than being loved,
however the plot comes out.
                              The soprano alive
at the end of the last act? *Qu'est-ce que c'est?*
The young suppose it is sad, that their timing is off;
we know better, as Tatiana also
by this point understands. At the end, her charm
is that she has married the prince, is rich beyond reach,
so he may echo her songs of desire and pass
to the world, and himself, as straight.
                                        It is entertaining
to be adored and to spurn—for his own good—
his absurd advances. Revenge may have some note
in the complicated score, but we may imagine
Tatiana at least toys for a time with the notion
of miracles and conversion: all he needs
is the love of a good—and sufficiently attractive—
woman! But no, that's nonsense, as she knows,
from that Liebestod of a duel. It was never her sister,
Olga, but Lenski, himself, with whom Onegin
flirted that night.
                    And now it is mostly tact,
or is she in this last scene, sentimental,
imagining how it might have been otherwise?
We do not have to choose: Tchaikovsky allows us
to come as close as we care to (or we dare to).
Laughter, suppressed and bitter enough, can hurt
as much as any of tragedy's bloody conclusions.
But Pushkin had it right: one can hear, offstage,
the jingle of the prince's spurs on the stairs
as he returns, lordly, boring, and real.

Authority

These fine discriminations are finally vexing;
the blather about this nuance or that,
this reading or that or, let's be frank, my reading
or others' (yours for example) erodes the spirit,
 wears one's patience away.
                         Toward the end of his life,
Rodzinski carried onto the podium always
a gun in his pocket, a small-caliber pistol,
not to be used or even brandished to threaten
the players, but felt, its heft there on the hip,
the pleasing sag of his trousers slightly askew:
a reassurance, a comfort. The cellos rasped?
The maestro could smile, imagine himself producing
 his baton's enforcer, and then the bang, the cry,
the blood, and at last, from survivors, assent, and the heavens'
music he heard in his head and had to struggle
to get from these overpaid, temperamental sons
of bitches, the bastards one has to make do with
for beauty's sake and art's.

The Gig

On a tippy table, here at the Penn State Days
Inn, I've been scribbling, mostly to pass the time. . . .
It's hardly what those would-be MFAs
imagine, or want to do, who think that I'm

curmudgeonly, or frivolous, or tired,
and resent being discouraged. And what if they do
get published and, on the strength of that, are hired
to teach creative writing (and one or two

sections of bonehead English)? Will I owe
apologies? Or will they also come
to such a pass and room as this and know
envy, resentment, and, worst of all, the numb

indifference that conspires with our own distaste
for readings in ugly lecture halls to sad
small groups, like all the others that we've faced,
impassive, if not sullen, ill read, ill clad,

as their instructors are, who never smile
or even get the jokes but talk of deals,
and publishers, and resent displays of style?
Why condescend to do it, then, if it feels

so bad, and worse all the time? One owes it to
the work? Of course not! But necessity
sneaks up from behind to bite you: you come through
to help a son with dentist's bills that he

can't manage. Therefore, I contrive a grin
with my own expensive teeth. I'll do my show-
and-tell and then get through the party in
my honor. Checking again the impossibly slow

minute hand of my watch, I'll long to get back
to this Days Inn and to quiet—my natural
habitat. Both flattery and attack
I shall endure with an abstract rictus and all

the grace I can muster, keeping my mouth shut,
for there's nothing to say, so long as they're hoping for
tricks of the trade—there are no tricks, and it's not
a trade. Imagine silence. A page turns. More

silence again. That's it. That's all there is.
And yet, from beyond the lamp's charmed circle, faces
are peering, the garish light of the lit biz
having lured them from their usual hiding places.

They're hungry for my secrets? Unearned income
is the most important; then, to have griefs like mine
for which there is no cure, though there can be some
respite with pen and paper's anodyne.

That's not what they want, is surely too much to handle,
but all I have, a gift not of my choosing,
and if no one seems to think it worth the candle
to learn to write well just to be amusing,

there's no help for them, or hope for their poems and
stories, those recitations, thinly disguised,
of betrayals they've suffered from parent or boyfriend
behaving badly. I was not surprised

by any trope or image of theirs. Then why
do they persist? What is the use? They are sad
poster children for some disease you and I
have never heard of. They have got it bad,

but I do, too, I suppose, am a chronic case,
no longer contagious, but that is what confuses
or even annoys. Too bad, but I'll leave this place
with a check for my son—worth a few new bruises.

An Extremely Short History of China

for Sophie Wilkins and Karl Shapiro

T'ang Dynasty

Suffering, suffering, squalor, suffering, flood, suffering, suffering, really severe suffering, war, suffering, suffering, drought, famine, suffering, brutal suffering, really terrible suffering, a slight diminution of suffering, a few years of reasonable life, the birth of some hope, the revival of the arts and crafts, and then corruption, disaster, war, and flood, drought, and more suffering.

Five Dynasties Era

Suffering, suffering, squalor, suffering, flood, suffering, suffering, really severe suffering, war, suffering, suffering, drought, famine, suffering, brutal suffering, really terrible suffering, a slight diminution of suffering, a few years of reasonable life, the birth of some hope, the revival of the arts and crafts, and then corruption, disaster, war, and flood, drought, and more suffering.

Sung Dynasty

Suffering, suffering, squalor, suffering, flood, suffering, suffering, really severe suffering, war, suffering, suffering, drought, famine, suffering, brutal suffering, really terrible suffering, a slight diminution of suffering, a few years of reasonable life, the birth of some hope, the revival of the arts and crafts, and then corruption, disaster, war, and flood, drought, and more suffering.

Yüan Dynasty

Suffering, suffering, squalor, suffering, flood, suffering, suffering, really severe suffering, war, suffering, suffering, drought, famine, suffering, brutal suffering, really terrible suffering, a slight diminution of suffering, a few years of reasonable life, the birth of some hope, the revival of the arts and crafts, and then corruption, disaster, war, and flood, drought, and more suffering.

Ming Dynasty

Suffering, suffering, squalor, suffering, flood, suffering, suffering, really severe suffering, war, suffering, suffering, drought, famine, suffering, brutal suffering, really terrible suffering, a slight diminution of suffering, a few years of reasonable life, the birth of some hope, the revival of the arts and crafts, and then corruption, disaster, war, and flood, drought, and more suffering.

Ch'ing Dynasty

Suffering, suffering, squalor, suffering, flood, suffering, suffering, really severe suffering, war, suffering, suffering, drought, famine, suffering, brutal suffering, really terrible suffering, a slight diminution of suffering, a few years of reasonable life, the birth of some hope, the revival of the arts and crafts, and then corruption, disaster, war, and flood, drought, and more suffering.

Republic of China

Suffering, suffering, squalor, suffering, flood, suffering, suffering, really severe suffering, war, suffering, suffering, drought, famine, suffering, brutal suffering, really terrible suffering, a slight diminution of suffering, a few years of reasonable life, the birth of some hope, the revival of the arts and crafts, and then corruption, disaster, war, and flood, drought, and more suffering.

People's Republic of China

Suffering, suffering, squalor, suffering, flood, suffering, suffering, really severe suffering, war, suffering, suffering, drought, famine, suffering, brutal suffering, really terrible suffering, a slight diminution of suffering, a few years of reasonable life, the birth of some hope, the revival of the arts and crafts, and then corruption, disaster, war, and flood, drought, and more suffering.

Transatlantic Flight

When it is now there, it will be then here,
but it is not now there yet.
Later it will be now there;
then it will be then there.
But then it will not be then here,
and then it will not be then there
or anywhere, ever again.

Cape Cod Snapshot

1

On dunes I've walked, a small girl picks her way
through clumps of beach grass, giving no special thought
to winds that send her red hair streaming, for wildness
is everywhere. She knows she must watch her step.

The way the picture is organized, with the small
white dress in the center of green grass
and dun sand and red hair against the deep
blue of beach sky, is arresting. She

is beautiful. That she happens also to be
my granddaughter is almost beside the point,
which is that the space is all but overwhelming;
that the wind, indifferently tousling hair and grass,

is dangerous; that we must snatch from its powerful
jaws whatever we can. Our eyes are down,
like hers, to find a path, but we look up
at such moments as this. The photograph

enlarges, one might say who didn't claim
kinship, as I do. But I wasn't there, could not
have pressed a button to freeze or seize this image
from the slipstream of her hurtle through childhood.

That intent look on her face comes to me finished,
as if I were a stranger. I must deconstruct,
reconstruct, and claim it. I stare at it hard
with swimming eyes, and try to enter the picture,

to pick my way with her among the hazards
of height, of sea's and sky's vertiginous space,
as winds blow our hair and billow our skirts'
composure. . . . How can one breathe in all that air?

2

She's long gone, that smallness shrunk to a speck,
floating, drifting out of the field of vision.
That sand has been smoothed to glittering blankness except
for this photograph, which helps to even the score

I keep in my head, a running tally of wrongs
like waves that break on the beach below her feet,
not without effect as they eat it away,
cut new channels, erode the Cape, erase it

as I should like to do. I reach for a pen
to work once more the trick of a giant squid
with tentacles and black ink—reach out, clutch
to my greedy head another delicious morsel

the current has offered or others have let slip.
This last word, always mine, may be a hollow
triumph, distorted, even a joke at my own
expense, but if a child takes up a pencil

and plays the vandal, drawing in a mustache
and big glasses, he signs the image, turns it
around, undoes stern faces that loom, and tames them,
as well as he can, to the harmlessness of toys.

from **PS3569.L3**
(1998)

Wonder Rabbi

for Deborah

So, nu?
What he knew! Ah, you
couldn't imagine, couldn't begin to begin
to imagine. To say he knew
the Talmud would miss the point. He knew it through
and through. But more than knew.
He was the book, had translated it to himself
and himself to it, to own it and be owned.
Listen, if you would open to any page
and let a straight pin touch on a word and then,
heaven forbid, push, so that it went through,
he knew, page after page, that sage,
that remarkable Jew,
what word your pin would pierce, would know, even feel
in his nerves the penetration of that steel
and he could explain to the men who stood around
in wonder what the words would be in order,
and give an interpretation that showed the real
meaning of their conjunction this way, reveal
the secrets that were hidden there, profound
and ancient mysteries, and make you, too,
for the moment at least rich in understanding.
Such, anyway, were the stories the old folks told
of what he could do,
that rabbi, when he was only seven years old.

Rudiments

In a darkness that children fear,
she is turned to a child again
as if time could reverse itself
or, abandoning now and then,
 just stop, having given up
on very old women and men.

Words, too, are blurred, but she keeps
a careful track of space:
the route from her chair to the kitchen,
the bathroom, her bedroom. Her face
is a map of the perils she gropes through
like furniture out of place.

In the afternoons, her daughter
comes to sit by her each day
for an hour. Their talk is awkward,
repetitive. . . . What they say is
beside the point, but her hand
on her daughter's knee that way

is soothing. She's waited for this
all day, and what agitates
or distresses her, though it remains,
at least for a while abates.
The daughter prepares her dinner,
feeds her, and washes the plates.

Then the ghosts return in their shifts
that are endless. The practical nurse
is frightened, but so is my aunt,
who may moan sometimes or curse,
or simply refuse to speak
in a rage that is even worse.

I think of them there, and weep,
and try not to rail against
how things turn out, and yet,

when I am depressed or tense,
at the end of my tether, I think
of those two and the rudiments

of courage and love in the mute
pressure and warmth of the touch
they exchange. It keeps them going.
It's what a life comes to, such
a gesture, a respite. O Lord,
how little it is, and how much.

Desk Set

1

By some trick of light or grace
the forlorn commonplace,
abruptly enriched, will appear
to be waiting for its Vermeer

to demonstrate what we've not
ever completely forgot. . . .
Look at some desktop trinket
you've had for years; you may think it

lucky or charmed: it is much
deeper than that, for your touch
inheres, suggesting this
is what the whole universe is

or would have been, had you tamed it,
conquered it, somehow claimed it.
But after the flood or the fire
what remains of that empire

and its generations of men?
This paper knife, this pen,
or blotter or pencil cup,
to show that it wasn't made up.

2

The string of my worry beads
frayed, gave way. I had to have the beads
restrung—and have to worry now about the beads themselves,
which ought to have functioned as emblems
without assuming, without presuming . . .
They impose themselves now as an independent subject
of worry: thirty-three beads and a marker bead.
They have some Islamic significance,
although I bought them in spite of that,
which is, I suppose, another reason to worry.

What does Islam know that the rest of us don't?
Are there only thirty-three worries? Are you hungry,
are you thirsty, are you cold, have you had a good bowel movement recently,
will you dream you are falling but, this time, not wake, actually hit, and die
    upon impact?
And so forth, for twenty-eight other categories of concern . . .
What sage or lunatic came to this abstruse reckoning? And was he
right? Was Spinoza right? Or Leibnitz? (That can't be a worry!)
There must be a miscellaneous category, which enables
but also defeats the entire system. What if
my jeweler calls, tells me the beads are restrung,
and I go and get them, only to find that I have nothing left to worry about, and
    have wasted my money
having had them restrung? I pray
for a life in which that could be a legitimate source of worry.
I cannot imagine such a life, but I am already vertiginous with envy
of the protagonist of my sudden fiction. . . .
The worry beads are blue and white, irregular, and nicely
nubbly to the touch. It is comforting to flick them with one's thumb.
That's an answer, albeit not a sufficient one. But what was the question?
All, yes, Leibnitz' first name—was Gottfried,
which is one less thing to worry about, except that I am likely to forget it,
which is deplorable but one of the consequences of getting older, and another,
    and slightly more serious subject for concern.

3

The print shows Harlequin, leaning, hovering over
recumbent Columbine. Behind him gauzy
curtains of tall French windows billow, looming
as Harlequin's outstretched wand swags them cloudlike.
On the ornate, pale blue chaise in the foreground, the girl
in ballerina's dancing slippers and tutu
appears to be sleeping—her dreams also cloudlike.
On the back, on the label age has foxed, I read
"Framed Specially for R. H. Macy & Co.,"
and below, in Palmer-method script, "Goodnight
Columbine" and then the name of the artist,
one "W. E. Webster." Nothing of interest,

except that my mother one afternoon must have paused,
must have been drawn to this once, her hand, her fancy,
hovering over that bin and lighting here.
Something I'm looking at now but cannot see
called out to something in her—the clown, the sleeping
girl, the open window, the wand, the curtains.

The title is odd. In the print, he is not leaving,
but coming in to wake her and turn her dream
sweetly, lovingly real. That upheld wand
is unambiguous, surely, as is the opened
window through which he has gained entry. Would mother
have known? Would she have needed or wanted the prudish
title? If she noted it, would she have thought it
mere good manners, or else seen through it? Ignored it?
It hung on the wall, in the hall as I remember,
above the Queen Anne bench. . . . Or was that a mirror?
The whole house has blurred. I dream of returning,
but the train breaks down, or the car, and I have to shift,
to improvise—I wade through thick muck, frightened,
exhausted. . . . These are nothing like Columbine's dreams,
whose name suggests the dove that betokens peace.
The scene is impossible: he is invisible; only
she can see him—or so the story goes—
which means that she has dreamt him, summoned him up,
wand and all. Hers is the magic, and he
is her sprite, an Ariel mostly but Caliban too,
and like them, almost tame. Most women think
we're something like that.
                              My father in that silly
suit? But forget the clothes and note the longing,
that representation of Harlequin's tender gaze,
the love.
              I say her fingers, flipping through prints,
froze there in pleasure or recognition, and chose.

4

                    In a line from an old screenplay,
                    a man in a ship's café

asks a sodden black-tied roué,
"What does your wristwatch say?"
who, after a moment's delay,
replies in a deadpan way:
    "Ticktock, ticktock."

A joke, but not merely, for those iterated sounds are
consonants that give definition to time's howling vowels,
a ululation, a moaning the wind might make in its wildness
over the sea or the rolling expanses of desert, its drawn-out
primitive vocalise, necessary but hardly
sufficient for what we are proud to define as civilization.

Monks, soldiers, the men of routine hacked out their hours
of prayers and watches. The sailors, otherwise lost, demanded
a further precision by which to reckon their longitude—
therefore, chronometers, and all their heirs, our pocket watches,
wristwatches, atomic clocks, the microtome slicers
of time's not-quite-infinite sausage. The two timepieces

that adorn my desktop accuse me of wasting what they dole out,
never quite in synchronization. Perfect
devices with their quartz hearts would be cheaper than these complex
machines with springs, gears, escapements, balances, and such
paraphernalia as the industrial revolution adored. One,
an old silver Tavannes that hangs on its stand, I bought

on impulse during the three weeks or so I worked for Otto
Preminger, and tempus, it tells me, sure does fugit.
The other watch, a gift from my mother-in-law, an old-fashioned
railroad Elgin, used to belong to her father—who did
time. No one speaks of this, but from what I gather and guess,
some construction project went bad, the gouging and graft too much

for even gaudy and greedy San Francisco. My wife's
grandfather took the fall (isn't that what Jews were for?).
Cigars (I've got his gold matchbox too) and the good
high life of the inside deals made and unmade him—
this instrument ticked off moment by raffish moment. Its taint
remained, somehow, and, several years ago, when a thief,

athletic or desperate, climbed our roof to break in at my second-
story window, what he grabbed from the desk was only this watch.
Distressed by the loss of a kind of heirloom, I never told
my mother-in-law what had happened, but six months later, I heard
the major crimes division was having an exposition
of stolen property they had recovered and I went down,

despite the impossibly long odds, to look—to avoid
the guilt of not having tried. Among yards of watches, cameras,
bracelets, rings, gold chains, and other tawdry valuta,
loot from the war that never lets up between rich and poor,
or poor and poorer, I took my turn with the rest of the victims,
avoiding one another's eyes, ashamed of ourselves

as unlucky ones, the fools who could neither accept nor let go.
In hell, I imagine, processions of damned souls search like this
for what they had taken for granted, like health, like air, until
they lost it—virtue, innocence, faith, and love, the key
to the garden, the childhood toy, the token, the icon. The odds
are long. . . . But there it was, my watch! Two years went by

until, just before trial, the fence's lawyer worked out
a deal, and copped a plea. The policemen could then give back
the watch they'd held in their evidence safe, that jail for objects
from which only luck had contrived a way to spring it. It keeps
good time (but what other kind is there?) as each
day unwinds and we watch each other's running down.

5

The green bronze cat is Ptolemaic. A god . . .
I used to know of what, but for me, it means
folly and how, on rare occasions, with luck,
it may be forgiven, even rewarded. I bought it
twenty years ago, in a shop in Cairo . . .
having no idea that shopkeepers there could report
such sales, turn in their customers, get a reward
from the government. Smuggling such antiques affronts
the nation and, of course, is against the law.
I'd bargained, perhaps too hard, but he had approved.

It's the ones who agree too soon for whom his contempt
must prompt dropping the dime, or whatever coin
informants use there. Later, out at the airport,
with my cat stashed in a suitcase, I was too nervous
to wonder why the porter was so insistent,
and, not having spent quite all my Egyptian money,
gave him a pound—worth seventy cents or so—
to deal with the bags. He accepted the limp bill
and chalked a mark on my luggage: I had cleared customs.
The pound, of course, was right. To have given nothing
would have been provoking; giving more, if I'd thought to,
would surely have aroused suspicion. A pound
was exquisitely calibrated baksheesh. Not
by sophistication, or any savoir vivre,
but only by grace had I been saved. Cold sweat
prickled my back in the transit lounge as I waited,
thinking of what could have happened, of what could still
happen. Then the plane boarded, taxied, took off. . . .
I waited to hear the landing gear retract,
signaling I was safe. . . .
                              But the cat god reminds me
I was lucky that time, and no one is ever safe.

6

There are many pens,
as if each one
had its own voice
and I could make
a considered choice
among them, but
whichever I take
I grope and stammer,
forget how to spell
and even my grammar.
But still they beckon,
gleaming gold,
silver, and black,
some new, some old,
inviting my hand

to remove the cap
of one of them and
venture once more
a word, a phrase.
Sometimes it works,
and I forget
myself and become
a child again,
or an inert accessory
of the pen.

≈

One is, in fact, solid gold,
the kind of pen that diplomats
use to sign treaties. . . . I like it
because it works as a touchstone does
but in reverse. If I know while I'm writing
with it that, yes, this is gold, expensive . . .
the words are probably worthless. But
if the pen disappears, turns into a plastic
Paper Mate or a Bic, then what
I am writing may not be without value.
One is my father's ancient Duofold,
green—it looked like malachite once.
Its cap still does, but the pen converts,
the nub at the end comes off, and instead
of a pocket fountain pen, it can serve
with its tapered quill in a stand, and did
for years on the desk in my father's office.
Years of sweat and sunlight faded
the green to a pale, ghost color, a ghost's
hand has never quite let go of.
I use it but only rarely, pretending
to be a grown-up, trying to pass
myself off as reliable, wise. . . .
I am intimidated by it,
used it to write the checks for my children's
tuitions. I used it to sign my will.

7

Other toys and baubles: a lapis lazuli
water buffalo, not Yeats' scholar's mountain
but not bad—a cow and her calf, and her horns
must have been hell to carve; a small Santa Clara
bowl, its lustrous black the result of the burning
horseshit they use, because wood is scarce, to fire
their almost useless pottery (water would melt it);
a peacock in cloisonné; a pretty inlaid
wooden stamp dispenser; an almost worthless
pocketknife I found years ago in the driveway
of the Cape Cod house—which is all I have left of it now;
a cheap dagger—its blade's braggart inscription:
"Never draw me without reason nor sheath me
without honor." I worry about that "nor."
A couple of goose-quill pens in a shot-filled holder.
A calculator. A magnifying glass.
They all hold their breath, attend, waiting with patience
that only objects know, who are sure they'll outlast
my whims and tastes, my history. Then, set free,
they will skitter away, dispersing to heirs, antique stores,
or trash heaps as would any flock of pigeons
after the bread crumb scatterer has gone.

The Art of Translation

Suppose that every tree translates
the wind into its idiolect, timbres
of differing timbers. Redolent now of pine pitch,

now of gum, or the duff of the oak grove,
it cleanses itself as fresh as when it arose
from the puffed-out cheeks of the ancient god.

In town, each gable and chimney modifies it
however slightly, enriching with commentary
and interpretation a never-changing text,

which is, however, without such impedimenta
mute and without such bodies unembodied.
Performance is, perforce, a misconstruction,

but better than none. As consonants drop away
the vowels will howl the same in your mouth or mine,
in a babe's or sage's: ooooh, eeeee, and aaaaah!

The Exigency of Rhyme

It distracts the mind to allow
for an openness, somehow
holding a thought but not
being held by it or caught
in its implication as we
otherwise surely would be. . . .

      Better yet, I remember a door-to-door Bible salesman who,
      when business was bad, would offer the rubes he sold the Good Book to
      his "autographed Bibles." "Signed by Jesus Christ? No way!"
      "Of course not, lady! I signed them myself," the salesman would say,
      "but look at that writing. It's plainly not my fist. I swear
      on a stack of my own fine product that the Holy Spirit is there
      guiding my hand when I do it." And the skeptical prospect pales,
      as often as not, and the drummer writes up one more of his sales
      of expensive Bibles with leatherette binding, a ribbon, and maps
      of the Holy Land in the back—and a signature that perhaps
      isn't quite his own. Which is what we poets can also claim,
      though few of us go so far as to substitute for our name
      the Lord of Hosts' or an angel's or one of those shoemaker's elves'
      without whose help we could never have said such things ourselves.

As If

"And does the defendant have anything to say?"
As the judge peers down from the bench, the well-read villain
replies he didn't really mean it literally.
His honor, laughing, imposes, nevertheless,
a sentence the malefactor may, if he likes,
consider as metaphoric, those long years
a mere figure of speech, for what is time,
or space, or even, for that matter, matter?
The oncologist's pronouncement, however grave,
is also a semiotic gesture, a mordant
trope from which the patient abstracts himself,
the point of the conversation as likely as not
being the way the sunlight gleams on the doctor's
pen-stand, or how, with the prominent hairs of his eyebrows,
he resembles a huge bug. Flights of fancy?
Or glimpses of God's odd truth? It's a consolation,
Musil's notion that these are rhetorical figures ·
and the world is an analogue for something else,
an anodyne for the pain that may feel real
but that God cannot intend in a literal way,
unless Musil didn't mean "literally" literally.
Is the *New York Times* in code? In our search for meaning,
for clarity in this muddle, we suppose
the world may be a backdrop, an indication
of something going on elsewhere on the canvas
or beyond the frame where we are unable to see it.
There that tree that is painted falling falls
in the eerie silence philosophers frighten us with.
Does that improve our case or make it worse?
Never mind meaning; we settle gladly for pattern,
the tensions and resolutions of dance or music's
order of chords. For the reassurance of rhythm,
we invent a god to thank. The faint heartbeats
and the gentle up-and-down of my mother's breathing

as she held me at her breast . . . That's what I want,
literally, but can't ever have again
except by the mind's extension, despair's routine
contrivance, which, God knows, is worth the world.

The Emperor's Rejoinder

Nakedness is not, itself, the disaster,
but the moment of realization that, yet again,
I seem to have left my clothing somewhere . . . that's bad.
The cool aplomb in which I was somehow clad
deserts me. The truth of such dream scenes is exposed—
for the psyche, when it makes jokes, never strays far
from the literal. That others have had the identical
dream is cold comfort. The folktale relies
on this common nightmare, but omits, so as not to distress
small children, the obvious ending. The crowd's
laughter subsides at length, and no one takes notice
of how the emperor, furious, glares at the boy
who broke the spell and orders his household guards,
as I have done, myself, many times: "Kill him."

The Second Murderer

CLAR. *In God's name, what art thou?*
2ND MUR. *A man as you are.*
CLAR. *But not, as I am, royal.*
2ND MUR. *Nor you, as we are, loyal.*
　　—SHAKESPEARE

People assume it's a rank. Second lieutenant?
Fiddler? Mate? Why not, therefore, a second
murderer . . . ? Plausible, but incorrect,
and the implications are misleading. There's no
exam I'd sit for to be promoted, no
august committee before which I'd have to appear
to get to be first murderer. That is a different
calling altogether. We are not like them,
not, if I may say, hotheaded, fanatic. . . . To be
neutral, let us call it *engagé*.
Your first murderer has a cause, an end
to justify his means. He cares, you see.
We are more balanced, reasonable people.
To us, it's a job, unpleasant perhaps, but jobs
often are. Your first murderer goes at it
with fervor in his heart, on principle.
We, less grandiose, are mostly after
profit, one way or another. Like most of you.
　　　　Another misconception has us
second murderers not so much assistants
as bumblers, oafs—but if we were so inept,
why would they need us? And they do, indeed,
need our presence. Committed as he may be,
your first murderer's not an expert, requires
help, more often than not, to get the job done.
More important, a second murderer changes
him from an undistinguished killer and mere cutthroat
to a leader. Now, it's a project, an enterprise
with a mission statement, an organizational plan,
and all that fine administrative framework
to disguise, a little, the unattractive truth.

Why else risk taking a witness along?
It's not an excursion. Nobody ever says:
"I'm off to kill the Duke of Clarence. Join me?
And afterwards, perhaps a spot of supper . . . ?"
Nevertheless, there is a social dimension,
a need he has for complicity, to share
that burden of guilt he'd otherwise bear himself.
I think it's a kind of marriage—for each of us, knowing
the other's secret, can bring him down. Joined now,
made kin to us by that blood we have shed together,
he knows he's never absolutely alone.
A danger, it's also a comfort, or was once. . . .
Now, with your Oswalds and your Sirhan Sirhans,
it doesn't cross their minds to recruit one of us.
Why? My guess for what it's worth is that guilt
has spread so wide that no assassin worries
in the night's dark moments lest he be the worst man
alive in the world. He's crazy, but not enough
to feel cut off from mankind—not these days.
I'm semi-retired. But I still keep my beeper.

Tryma

A tryma is a nutlike drupe.
No one in your playground is likely to respond
to such an observation in any reasonable way, but
you can always explain that a drupe has a single endocarp,
which is true but not, perhaps, helpful.

A pneuma is, by extension, a breathlike trope?
That, we may agree, would be horsing around, but
a drupelet, which is a small drupe, as, for example, the pulpy grain of the blackberry,
would have, logically, an endocarplet.
When it rains, as it may from time to
time, I can imagine you running
through the meadow exclaiming, "Ah,
see the droplets on the druplets!"

You will be an exquisite child,
or, rather, are already, but you will proclaim it
in such a way as to defy the world.
And will they call you on the carplet?
Defy them, defy them.

The trauma of the tryma
is with us always, as are the poor
in spirit, who will stare at you blankly
or in resentment ask,
"Wha'? Who?"
Answer them smartly and tell them
the wahoo is a kind of euonymus
(which is a good name)
with arillate seeds.
Tell them your grandfather said so.
If that doesn't work, and it won't, you can take some comfort
from knowing that the false aril originates
from the orifice instead of the stalk of an ovule
as in the mace of the nutmeg, which is an arillode.

It follows, I suppose, that a true aril is a false arillode,
although people seldom say so,
but never let that stop you.

Domitian at Ostia

When the sun glints bright
and the breeze is right,
        one is prompted then to go
and put out to sea
where the soul can run free
        at least for an hour or so.

When the day is clear,
one thrills to hear
        how the rigging snaps in the ship's
spars, while the stays
hum their hymns of praise.
        You can also hear the whips

as the galley slaves
dip their oars in the waves
        to the tunes the bo'sun sounds,
and our wake's white scud
is flecked with blood
        from their randomly crosshatched wounds.

Oh, it's splendid to ride
an outgoing tide,
        and the heart of a sailor soars
like a great seabird
for his having heard
        that rhythmic splash of the oars.

When the sun glints bright
and the breeze is right,
        one is prompted then to go
and put out to sea
where the soul can run free
        and sail for an hour or so.

from **Falling from Silence**
(2001)

Height

The question that he frames in all but words
is what to make of a diminished thing.
　　—ROBERT FROST

My doctor, for some obscure reason, is checking
not only my weight but (he's kidding, right?) my height. . . .
This is for pediatricians, and parents who mark
the growth of their little darlings on door frames. But now
he adjusts the metal rod to the top of my head
and discovers a diminution. I am not, he tells me,
six feet anymore, but five feet ten and a half. . . .
And what (aside from the obvious wise-ass answer)
is the difference?
　　　　　　　I'm not—as I was, as I thought of myself—
tall. I was proud of that height I'd done nothing to earn.
If it simply happened, whatever talent I have
also just happened, as grace does, or love. And now
it's gone. As grace can go, or love. And we do
what we can to accept and adjust. (What choice do we have?)
I'm average. Of middling stature. I stand up as straight
as I can, the way I was taught to do as a boy,
but it doesn't help, won't change me, can't bring back
that not altogether insignificant edge
I used to have. With this slight shift in perspective,
no longer *de haut en bas*, there may be new lessons
I apparently need to learn in humility, faith,
or simply that resignation that age should provide.
A tall order, it may yet come in time.

The Upas Tree

Wherever it is—if it is, that is—then that
is the middle of nowhere, its lonely habitat,
the ground around it, desolate and bare.
No songbird ventures near its poisoned air;
no bush or fern can grow, or blade of grass—
only itself, the upas tree, which has
such toxic power that nothing else will thrive
within a ten-mile radius or survive
in five, they say, whoever *they* are. Who?
Natives with tales of fools who ventured too
far upriver and, with a tortured breath,
spat warnings of that tree and the terrible death
with which it punishes any who come too close
to the empty place in the jungle where it grows.
A fabrication, perhaps, to keep us out
who have come to exploit and enslave their country? No doubt,
but are we not also intrigued and attracted by
the idea of such a thing and inclined to defy
the natives' superstition? Shall we not go
upcountry, therefore, and paddle for days in the slow,
muddy current, peering at each bend to see
through a gap in the jungle's wall that fabulous tree,
serene in the noxious beauty we can assume
so deadly a thing must have, and a rich perfume
its enormous blossoms pour into empty air
in a vain abundance, for nothing else is there?
In that glade's unholy silence, day and night,
it contemplates itself in a Carmelite
devotion even heaven might envy, sick
of generation and all that spawning of thick
swarms of life so avid for being. This
rejection of the world's abundance is
the exquisite idea that each may reach
after learning all that affirmation can teach.
It is the jungle's dream of the tundra's bare
and gelid abnegation, satiety's prayer
to which we all must say Amen one day.

Upriver, inland, where all the maps give way
to featurelessness, there are many stories told
of abandoned cities or mountains of pure gold,
obvious in their appeal to the vulgar mind,
which is reason to disbelieve them. More refined
and different is that of the upas, which some men
have wondered about and even believed in. When
we approach it, our breathing bated, do we feel
the body's ebbing away? It has an appeal
we never expected but come to appreciate
as we yield ourselves to the single-minded hate
at the root of that tree, its defiance, rejection, and curse
upon everything alive in the universe,
including itself—but, being immune to its own
poison, it has to keep going, albeit alone,
until, one day, there may come from a grudging sky
the lightning bolt it awaits, and it, too, can die.

The Weight of the Spirit

With much glass tubing and flashing arcs, the not-
quite loony doctor in his white coat essays
the problem of spirit and matter: he has got
enormous delicate scales on which he weighs

the dying and dead, hoping thus to find
by how many grams or grains it is that the spirit,
departing, diminishes corpses. Or ask whether mind
weighs a bit more than the dead brain does (I fear it

may be a different but similar question)? Still,
I brood about these things, often late at night.
As I'm drifting off, there's an inner self that will
settle, palpably falling away to the right

and behind me—no matter how I am lying in bed.
A smaller, simpler creature, rather better
than I am, it is not quite happily wed
to me, or is stuck with me, or to me. Let our

selves be startled, as when we say we've had
a turn, and I can feel it try to adjust.
I am the baggy suit through which the sad
clown must display his grace in that sawdust

where elephants just performed. Sometimes in panic,
it loosens its grip, or, very rarely, in bliss.
When I am not quite myself, depressed or manic,
I feel its letting go. What remains of me is

negligible, and knows it, is bereft
and at the same time indifferent. It obeys
instructions the departed spirit left
before it left. Exactly what it weighs,

those scientists never determined. As soon ask why
when a magnet is demagnetized, the metal's

loss is only of meaning. When I die,
I'll know the feeling, as my spirit settles

into its final rest for that long night—
behind me and a little to the right.

Privately Owned

for John Fitz Gibbon

At night, on the walls of a house, its paintings dream,
or, say, play in the dreams of those who dwell
among them: on the walls of their minds they hang
or swim in the dark, but then, as a new day dawns,
coming up for air, they surface again to light
and settle into the frames where we think them fixed.

Domestic wildlife, they frisk, while those in museums,
caged, like Schopenhauer's ape or Rilke's
panther, stare down at blank and stupid guards
in whose stolen naps there is no room for greatness
to move in, never mind romp as they also do
in churches, where in parishioners' prayers, those directed

dreams, the shimmering marches of consciousness
offer that unconstrained attention they thrive in.
A glimpse is never enough, as the steady gaze
of scholars, too eager and earnest, is too much.
From a canvas, stretched over time, each stroke of the brush
must make its mark in the slowly roused neuron.

Each daybreak, and every passage along that wall,
indicts, corrects your memory, trains your eye
with tints, textures, and shapes that are not even better
but different, surely, from what you believed with surprises
ever smaller but nontheless precious for that,
like a many-years-married couple's allusive banter.

The Valve

The one-way flow of time we take for granted,
but what if the valve is defective? What if the threads
on the stem wear thin, or the stuffing box or the bonnet
ring leaks, or the joints to the pipe ring fail,
and there's a backwash?
                It happens.
                        And then old loves,
meeting again, have no idea what to do,
resuming or not resuming from where they were
years before. Or the dead come back to chat.
Or you are reduced for a giddy moment to childhood's
innocent incompetence. You look up
as if to see some hint in the sky's blackboard.
But then, whatever it was, some fluff or grit
that clogged the works, works free, and again time passes,
almost as before, and you try to get on with your life.

Airedales

Those who did it are dead now. And what they did,
they were trained to do and had no choice, no freedom.
Still, when I read in some book review that the camps'
guard dogs were "Alsatians, Airedales, and Doberman
pinschers," I can't help blaming the dogs of these breeds,
even though they have no idea what breeds they are.

Alsatians? Of course. And Dobermans? They are weapons
that sometimes wag their tails. But Airedales?
                                              Yappy
clowns they are, huge terriers after all.
Frisky perhaps . . . But then the zebra-suited
Musselmanner didn't think they were cute
as they watched the attacks of those packs of killer dogs.

But the National Association for the Advancement
of Airedales? And the Airedale Anti-Defamation League?
And the liberal line that says I cannot blame
a class for what some members may have done?
They are all correct, as I admit at once.
But I would cross the street to avoid an Airedale.
And I would not have an Airedale in my house.

A Zemerl for Rabbi Nachman

1 Rabbi Nachman Goes into the Woods

He would go, in his brokenheartedness, into the woods
every day, as if he had an appointment
to talk for an hour to God, speaking in Yiddish,
or maybe not speaking, but only repeating one word,

or less than a word, a syllable, a single
vowel, a howl, a pure vocalization,
from which he expected little result. "Zimzum,"
God's apartness or, say, His withdrawal, requires

drastic, desperate measures, and Rabbi Nachman's
keening out in the woods he believed would work
like water that can wear away a stone.

The stone, he said, is the heart—not God's, but his own,
which little by little he might contrive to soften,
to open again, soothed, or even healed.

2 The Rabbi in Town

But in town, what? In Bratslav or Zlatipolia,
surrounded by crowds? What can one do?
                                        Try
to take some comfort: a single person's prayers
God may reject; but in shul, in a minyan, bound up
with the prayers and the hearts of the others, surely the Lord
will hear your supplication.
                            And when that idea
 fails to comfort?
                    Then, as the Rebbe said,
"One can dance such a small and delicate dance
that no one can see. And also one can scream
in a still, small voice, making a great scream
that no one else can hear, without a sound,
a scream in the silence, a scream your mind imagines
that penetrates your being. And all being."

3 Equity

Knowing how bad he feels, how much he grieves,
how sharply aware he is of the separation
between himself and God (all knowledge starts
from this), he extorts from this terrible absence
a consolation, extrapolating, to think
how it has to be, at the other end, much worse
for God, who must also grieve cut off from him.

4 Mirrors

The face of the moon reflects the sun's bright light;
so a disciple's face must receive and mirror
the enlightenment of his master, for it is written
in Scripture how the Lord spoke "face to face."*

And the master beholds himself in his pupil's face:
imagine two mirrors in opposition
with their infinite repetitions of one another. . . .
But this, Rabbi Nachman said, only partly in jest,
would be displeasing to heaven. "If God were content
to worship Himself, what need would He have of us?"

5 The Telling of Stories

Science? It comes from the forehead of the snake.
And Reason? The Rebbe called it an imperfection:
for a man to be whole, he must learn to let go, be simple,
and in his descent ascend to faith and joy.

These are subversive ideas that evil men
seize upon and misuse. Therefore, he contrived
a way to reveal his teachings while keeping them hidden—
in stories. Here he could fashion a garbing of wisdom
to trick the unwary. And good for good men, too.
To waken the sleeping spirit, one must go slowly.
Think how it is when a blind man is healed: they give him
a blindfold; they have to protect him from too much light

*Deuteronomy 5:4

that could ruin his sight.

In this he had changed his mind.

A younger man, he had fought against fantasy's dangers,
its snares and delusions distractions from truth and faith;
but fantasy, too, is a power that comes from God.

The struggle is not against the imagination
but within its extravagant realm, in its heights and depths.

6 The Tale of the Man Deep in Debt

The money itself is the least of it. (Still, the amount
you owe is more than you have or can ever hope for.)
It's the shame that oppresses, the fact that you're forced to admit
you're a failure, a fool, have been weighed and found wanting. Poor,
you are, as the world reckons, of no account,
a zero, worthless, of negative worth, an abject
object of scorn and derision your neighbors point to,
warning their sons not to grow up to be like you.
Of that shame, he was connoisseur; of that utter dejection
he was the master. In stories a man tells
are the snares his heart has thrashed in, and Rabbi Nachman's
woe is here in its richness.

"And then what happens?"

is the question we learned as little children to ask.

The rabbi tells us how the poor man at last
is brought in his shame and terror into the office
where the rich moneylender to whom he owes more than his all
sits and hears him out as he stammers excuses,
lame, unpersuasive even to his own ears
as he mouths the bitter words.

But the terrible judgment

does not come. Instead, the man waves his hand,
explains he has millions, and says that he doesn't care.
The debt is trivial, nothing to worry about,
and the poor debtor feels both relieved and insulted.
The rich man, seeing this, as an act of kindness
suggests, "There is a way you might work off
the debt, for others owe me sizable sums.

If you will go to my other debtors, remind them
their payments are overdue, and try to collect,
you will bring me hundreds of times what you owe. Agreed?"
Of course.

It's the *rebbe*, the man who owes—not money
but a moral debt. And the moneylender is God,
blessed be He. And this is how, with his defects,
Nachman presumes to preach and teach, to remind
us others how much we owe, and to whom, and how
we ought perhaps to consider some partial payment.

Angel of Death

An abrupt silence no deaf man could dream of,
a sudden darkness no blind man could fear,
and a breathlessness of a focused attention that fades . . .

I always supposed it would be like that. Now, weathered,
but hardly wiser, I cannot improve or refine
that child's idea of dying. It oughtn't be
subtle: even the stupid contrive in the end
to accomplish that mortal feat—falling off a log.
(But never hitting the ground, the fall going on
forever?) Something like this is what she sidles
up to, drifting off again to a nap,
as if for practice.
                            The tongue seeks out a tooth's
rough place, and the mind reverts to an irregularity,
as if by such usage to lick it smooth. It never
works; the snag persists; there's a run
in the future's nylons.

What's left in hand is not even good for rags.

        ✐

The name in Hebrew? My daughter-in-law is asking
so she can pray for her.
                            She never had one,
or never knew or doesn't remember.
(She doesn't remember a lot.)

For *Barbara? Bracha*, maybe? "Blessing"?
Or we could go for the meaning:
"stranger"—*Gershona*, the feminine version
of the name of Moses' son, who was
"born in a foreign land."
(And the patronym? Uncle Dick's
Hebrew name? We can get that
perhaps from her brother's headstone.)

Which of us here in this light is not a stranger?

Socrates said death is no misfortune.
Most men would like to believe this but cannot.
We bear the cost of language, which can suppose
whatever we like, or hate, or can imagine.
(And imagination is often of what is not.)

⪫

The terror is not in the dying but in the mind,
the brain—and hers is riddled, rattled, raddled,
radiated. She frets but cannot remember:
did she take her medicine? merely think to do so?
It makes no difference. She is beyond cure,
but not beyond care. . . .

        As if her survival
depended somehow on her being a good girl,
she thinks if she does what she's told, nothing bad
will happen to her.

        This is what she assumes
and has always lived by.

        It is not so.

⪫

Another stranger waits, meanwhile,
at the furry tent-flap. One day this week, or next,
he or she will appear and, in what looks like
rage, with small clenched fists will cry and blink.
And who can say it is not with cause?
Was it Sophocles or Hesiod who said,
"What is best is never to have been born"?
Both, I'm afraid.

⪫

Across a leaden sky, three arrowheads:
Canada geese, on their way south. How do they
know where they're going? How do they choose
their squadron leaders? I am on cruise control,

but so are they, tending better than I can
to destinies for which they cannot imagine
alternatives, and in their sure
purposiveness, would not, even if geese could.
I envy that, but my car, going up a hill,
shifts to maintain its speed. My body, too,
responds to its own system controls.
Mostly, I don't even know when it changes gear.
Those arrowheads have written on the sky . . .
A warning? A word of comfort?
                                        A statement of fact.
The baby, Barbara, and I are all in formation,
which is all the information anyone needs.
Do I believe that?

Does it make any difference what I believe?

        ⁓

The baby, due at the solstice, had to have been
conceived at the equinox—around my birthday,
as I would have been begun at the summer solstice.
Does that coincidence make us closer kin,
give us some special connection?
Not at all—unless one of us thinks so.

        ⁓

After a stillbirth, or after an infant death,
the next child, some primitive tribes believe,
is stronger, bearing both lives, its spirit cagey,
having been here a while already to scout the terrain.

It's true, of course, for these "replacement children"—
which is what they're called—get special love and attention,
a doting another child could never imagine.
They are, for the rest of their lives, princes, princesses.

And here, when a birth and a death coincide?
                                        It's hard
not to suppose some balancing out of accounts

as we see how, at almost the same moment,
the Lord giveth and taketh away.

Such consolations are stupid.

But better than none.

⁊ℴ

Barbara called last night: her right side
is weak, she has trouble walking, trouble
getting up out of bed.

This morning, when we telephone to ask
how she's doing, she can't remember
the call she made last night.
Trouble.
And twenty minutes later . . .
but this time it isn't Barbara.
Now it's Josh. From the hospital:
Nadine's water has broken.

⁊ℴ

For unto us a child is born.
Unto us a son is given.
And his name shall be called
Samuel.
My father's name. And Nadine's father's father's.
"Asked of God," as every child should be.

I hold him in my arms, the precious, breathing
weight, and admire the tiny hands
that will bear the weight one day of my coffin's corner.
Two sons and two grandsons . . . Thanks be to God.
That a Sam once more will carry me is a comfort.

⁊ℴ

But that's far off.
Barbara, who takes much shorter views,

receives my news with moderated pleasure.
"I'll try to remember," she says.

She has other things on her mind
(what's left of her mind)—
these unsayable things that I have been thinking.
She has been thinking, too. We are children again,
playing at musical chairs. The music is stopping.

Someone is taking her place.

꩜

This is also, I realize, my father's Yahrzeit. . . .
The first few years, I used to light a candle,
but I gave it up. Still, I would always feel
some twinge of guilt—enough to be annoying.
One learns to live with that; now I won't have to.
This is his candle, my grandson, his namesake,
shining with a new lifetime of light.

꩜

Time passes, a month, another. Barbara
has stabilized. "At a somewhat lower level
than we might have hoped," is how a doctor puts it.
With the help of a walker, she can get around her apartment.
Once, when the weather was good, she went to a movie.
Two men carried her down the stairs in a chair
and then, in the ambulette, to the movie theater,
and home again. She remembers the film and liked it,
but cannot think of the name. She complains of boredom.

꩜

We, too, are bored, but cannot say so. Grief
has its own pace and rhythm. We've moved along,
but she is stuck where she was, hangs on like a leaf
on a tree in winter, waiting, daring the wind.

Sam, meanwhile, has outgrown his first baby clothes.
Yesterday, he turned himself over, that first
assertion of will and control in a difficult world.

꩜

A plateau, the doctors call it, and yet it tilts
ever so slightly downward. As whose does not?
My birthday has come and gone and the vernal
equinox. It isn't Sam but myself
I think of. The burgeoning spring is his. For us
it is that time of the fall, exhilarating
but chastening, when we wait for the killing frost.

I am looking for this evening's concert tickets.
I am drinking coffee. I have been reading proof. I am
interrupted. The phone rings.

                            It is midmorning.
Early calls are frightening. Late ones, too.
Wrong numbers, as often as not. But the Angel of Death
telephones these days, and good news keeps
for a civilized hour.

Without apprehension, I answer.
The word from the hospice director: "deterioration."
Her right side's all but gone. She has "some pain"
in her back (which could be spinal mets). She is frightened.
The question is whether to hospitalize her now.
No, I say, because that would frighten her more.
The apartment is familiar. Keep her there.

Neither of us has spoken the other dire
word that hangs in the air,
but she will die at home.

꩜

"Deterioration" means:

        Catheterized. She has trouble otherwise
passing urine. It could be the pain meds.

It could be tumor, obstructing, somehow,
the urethra. Or neurologic, a difficulty
in getting commands through
from scrambled brain to wasted body.

       Bed-ridden. She fell again, was that sack
of meal I remember from a visit some months ago
when her legs gave way. Two passing Samaritans
helped me get her on her feet again.
That was before the walker, before the chairs,
motorized to help her stand up. Now,
she is in a hospital bed from which she will never
arise. In weeks or days, men in black suits
will carry that sack away.

    ❧

She is "agitated," afraid. And Ativan
doesn't work, or does "paradoxically,"
making her feel even worse. So what do they have
to fall back on? The next word in the curt
sentence is the grim relief, morphine.

    ❧

Monday night, on the phone, she cries, afraid.
Tuesday, I don't call. None of us does.

Wednesday, they call us to announce it's over.

Driving home from the end-of-the-term party,
I had seen, on the side of the road, a doe's carcass,
not fifty feet from one of those caution signs
with a bounding buck on a yellow diamond.
                                   Barbara's
plight, I thought. The signs do no damn good.
They tell us what we already know.

At home, a part of me knew, before I heard
the words, that Barbara was dead.
In her sleep, she just stopped breathing.

This morning, in the yard, the first iris
has opened, burst its green pod, showing forth
its royal purple flag, her favorite color.
Another sign? It could be, if I believed it,
but does that do me any good? Or her?

And then I catch myself. What I can believe
is grammatical rules. That present tense has departed
along with her and is wrong. All her verbs now
are in the imperfect, perfect, and pluperfect,
what she was, has been, what she had been.

Culls

1

What could I have been thinking? (Was it thinking?)

Fantasy, say, or an aspiration: to be
better read. To be better. More thorough, more
generous in my tastes and interests. But this
welter of books I will never look at again
in this life or any other a Shirley MacLaine
might dream up, coming back, time after time . . .

What's strange is the appetite I must once have had:
that voracity's gone now. The gift of age
is taste or, say, an exquisite distaste.

I cannot imagine ever wanting to look at
a poem of—for example—Donald Hall
or Peter Davison, or . . . (fill in the blanks).
By such honest judgments, exercised often,
these piles on the tops of bookcases, on floors,
even under chairs, might be at least reduced.
If I don't do it, my wife someday or my children
will have to paw through this incoherent heap.

Who wants it? Who could ever have wanted this?

An interrogative pause. And an unsentimental
declarative silence. With which one cannot argue.

On the shelf in my head are the few books I live with.
Chaucer's clerk of Oxenford had twenty,
which sounds about right. (Chaucer's is one of them, surely.)
The rest are failures, the writers' or mine, good manners
would prefer not to admit. Or else, like clothing,
say I have somehow outgrown them. The closet, too,
indicts with its profusion: what was I thinking?

2

The brain adapts. We can no longer memorize
as we used to do. In surfeit, it sulks, rejects
these projects we propose. But this sorting out
and throwing away, it knows and enjoys, the old
dog's new trick that it does all the time. To remember
every moment? Such unrelentingness
of indiscriminate consciousness prefigures
the torments of hell. (But for what we have let go
we can hope for forgiveness, and perhaps forgive ourselves.)

Which is getting close to the truth we try to avoid
however we can—that life, after all, is finite
and its range of possibilities, ever more narrow.

The light changes: the air is not yet chilly
but feels different; the green of the trees' leaves
is not what it was last week or yesterday,
and we are betrayed by the look of the land on a hillside.

I noticed that change indoors—it was years ago—
in bookstores, or it was in myself in bookstores,
the old eagerness bruised, the invitations
(theirs and mine) more tentative now, more guarded.

When nomads learned to farm and settled down
by a riverbank, cities were born, and soon thereafter
middens: those ancient places are layers of garbage,
and still when I walk the streets, I can feel them shifting
beneath my feet: under the blocks of solid
pavement that rubble heap, unstable, settles.

3

What will I re-read, or even consult?
Let us admit that, for all their heft on the shelves,
books are flighty, become souvenirs of themselves,
appealing no longer to intellect and taste
but playing to sentiment. Why else keep on hand
Look Homeward Angel, except in the hope that the schoolboy
who turned its pages may show up some afternoon?

And what would we have to say to one another?

Still, for his sake, I have lugged this book along
for years, packed and unpacked it, reshelved it, prepared
for a meeting such as I neither expect nor desire.

What remains when we've finished reading a book?
The impression is vague, like the aftertaste of wine
or the scent a woman was wearing that stays in the room
which seems to remember and then imagine her presence.
Such residues, I used to assume, compounded,
changing, enriching the reader. And an education
was what persists and accumulates. The figure
is homelier now: imagine a porcelain sink
that over the years hard water has stained; look up;
and see what wisdom the face in the mirror has earned.

Thus Mallarmé's disgust, when he said he'd read
all the books—it wasn't a boast, the remark
having begun by asserting that flesh was sad.

*Depression ... but that's a name for truth the doctors
can't admit (to us or themselves) they agree with.*

We learn its trick too well, how literature
can make the world make sense as we get to the end
and for twenty minutes after we've finished a book
when it all coheres. The harmonies of music,
its reliable resolutions, suggest the same
abstract affirmation. A new day dawns,
but insomniacs see that light as indictment, as judgment
of the body's betrayal and, worse, the spirit's failure.
It only reveals the full extent of disaster,
ruin far worse than anything we had imagined—
a hurricane, a flood, a plague, a pogrom.

4

More calmly, with better balance: I am not immortal;
I am not a repository library; I ought not
presume to impose my tastes on my wife or children

and grandchildren. And the books that I discard
I do not destroy but let free to go on their way
to a dealer's limbo to seek their fortunes—perhaps
to gain admission into their version of heaven,
that shelf of the right reader the author imagined.
For this, they were created. What else matters?

Keepers (or books to detain for a time): the tools
of the trade, the grammars, atlases, dictionaries,
and reference works I consult rather than read.
But the category blurs. To the Bible, Shakespeare,
Homer, Virgil, Ovid . . . one goes to look up
more often than just to sit and, in innocence, read,
innocence, being the lack of a purpose, question,
or practical prompting. Such motivations are base,
almost dishonest: we want to appear to know more
than we really do. What our fingertips find we let
people suppose we had on the tip of the tongue.

Then books of friends, and of writers I love: Nabokov,
Proust, Faulkner, Calvino, Nooteboom, Perec,
Raphael, Garrett . . . But fiction has moved upstairs,
mostly displaced by fact's more serious claims
to which, despite my behavior, I give no credence.
Poetry I keep close, in the room with my desk—
to consult or, say, confer with. For company. Prompting?
That, too. In a kind of conversation
I sometimes believe in, the work of others will speak
to elicit answering speech. Even here, sometimes,
I must cull to make room for what keeps coming in.

In the vigor of youth, reckless, we move or divorce,
and slough off, telling ourselves we will start again,
rebuild, improve, refine, but life isn't like that.
Disaster relents, while I flourish and thrive and the shelves
fill up. I ought to be pleased with such aggregation
like Blenheim's or Chantilly's—but mine is messy,
scattershot, impromptu—in character, too.
The bookshelves' burden remains pretty much what it was.
The occasions over the years have changed and the titles,

but inconstancy is the only constant: I see
my lack of focus and purpose, the same deplorable
flightiness I promised—how many times?—
I'd change and apply myself and pay attention . . .

Did my father ever believe my protestations?
Did I, even as I spoke, believe myself?

5

Even my own books accuse me, their silent
baleful reproaches an ever heavier burden:
I should have taken greater pains. More time,
more effort, and, face it, more talent, and I could have made them
better. Mostly I've learned to ignore them: the blurred
monument to my underachievement, the offspring
a dysfunctional parent has let loose on the world.
A few I don't dislike. And for some of the others
the small twinge of displeasure that they occasion
isn't their fault or mine but comes from the fate
we endured together—a signal unsuccess
I tell myself, with some degree of truth,
was the publishers' fault, the reviewers', the bookstore buyers',
the public's, the gods'. Across the street in a warehouse,
I have a locker piled high with the out-of-print
remainders I bought cheap but must pay to keep
(for whom?). A regressive tax levied on failure.

Still, for argument's sake, there must be a few
of that spawn I let loose on the world that found somehow,
against all odds, a home—like those spiders that spin
silk filaments on which they can float on the winds
across the Pacific's vastness. Most of them die
but a few find their remote atoll that luck
or fate had put there—a reef, a few palm trees
from the coconuts the tides had washed ashore,
the paradise their mad genes had predicted.

That home I like to imagine my books may find
is not in my house but in that of some amateur

not in the business, not a writer, reviewer,
editor, critic, or teacher—who every so often
has to do this, go through this dreary process
and cull. Instead, he keeps in his single bookcase
those few volumes he has made part of his life,
that speak to him somehow and in his head
resonate. And one of them is mine.

Two Prophets

for Bill Kent

A sacred calling, but both of them are mortals,
fallible, even foolish, and sooner or later
they meet, the two prophets—so Strabo says—
and in what may have begun in a friendly way,
swap tales, boasting of feats of prognostication:
Mopsus tells his stories for Calchas to match,
and it turns to a competition, each one daring
the other.
                Calchas points to a nearby fig tree
and asks how many he thinks there are.
                                        In an instant,
"Ten thousand less one," Mopsus answers,
"just enough to fill the hold of the ship
arriving at this moment, I do believe,"
and he points a hand vaguely toward the harbor.

A defiantly odd number. They hire a crew
to pick the tree clean, and sure enough,
9,999
figs, and they fit in the hold of the ship. Just.

Now it's Calchas' turn, and Mopsus asks,
"That sow about to farrow . . . Would you perhaps
hazard a guess? The number of piglets? Their gender?"
Calchas, who hasn't the vaguest idea, says so,
annoyed, because this shouldn't be a game.
But Mopsus, who isn't playing, announces, "Ten.
Tomorrow. One, a male, will be all black.
The other nine will be females, streaked with white."

And so it happens. And Calchas is undone.
Destroyed, he dies, we read, "in an excess of grief."

As if that business at Aulis were nothing. As if
the puzzling out of the plague at Troy had been nothing.
He is not the *Iliad*'s author or *Oresteia*'s
but he foretold all their bloody and grand events
which ought to have weighed in the scale

against . . . what?
Figs and pigs!
And the deadly worm of envy
that blinds and eats into the heart, that makes
even the profoundest wisdom partial.
What it can make, in the end, is a heavy heart.

≈

The future, we have learned in a hard school,
is misty. The past, where we look for what we love
or are proud of to find that it jostles with shame, is also
misty.
And who could bear it, otherwise—
clear, plain as day? We walk a knife-edge,
chasms on either side of us, and we learn
never to look down, or almost never.

≈

In the *Argonautica,* there is a similar duel:
Mopsus predicts, as it turns out quite correctly,
much of the bloody business they face and the bloody
consequences: Medea, the butchered babies.
But Idmon gets up and, although he leaves out a lot,
foretells success. There are tears running down his cheeks
the crew supposes are those of joy, but we know
better and comprehend their happy error.
We see what he can see: his death. Does Mopsus
resent Idmon's intrusion? Does he see, too?
Not told, we are not prevented from supposing
whatever we prefer or may find congenial.
But we are invited to make it a better story.

The lines in his palm the baby is born with map
the road his feet will travel, but do not peek:
even if you could tell the story, let him
find his own voice. The plot may be fixed
but he may contrive stylistic variations
no one could have expected by which he will change
everything, or better redeem everything,
or at least put it somehow into quotation marks.

Stare into his eyes and let what wisdom
your years have accumulated meet his hopes.
Can you say, positively, which of you is wrong?

This habit of leaning into the future is cruel.
Distinction is what we inherit or earn: our status
is always a gift of the status quo, our past
being what we are now. What we may become
is for preachers and politicians, the demagogues,
who threaten or promise. It does not own us yet.

Mopsus' showy tricks are irrelevant, vulgar,
a lounge act. A singer would do as well,
or even a poet, Calchas. But you were undone
nonetheless. It wasn't Mopsus but you,
your own doubts that required you, every day,
to prove again that you had the god's favor.

As if the gods were constant.
                              As if Apollo
had not, for a time, done duty as Admetos' shepherd.

Apollo knew who he was, but your faith, Calchas,
failed.
        As Mopsus guessed—or foretold—it might.

Beyond the lounge, you can hear the casino noises,
the pulling of cranks, the clatter of coins, the bells
when a jackpot hits. The "gaming industry"
isn't a game either. And the money is only
tokens.

What they yearn for, every one,
is the gods' favor. The smiling of fates that have heard
their prayers and been moved to answer. Lacking that,
what of worth can remain, or what other ruin
can matter?

There is no time, no day or night,
and the garish lights may stand for the stars or flash
like beacons beckoning, warning.

Those who have faith
do not require assurance. But we who doubt
and therefore want the gods, know sacrifice
is necessary—what we ourselves would demand
in the way of worship, penance, and punishment.
Cherries, bars, and lemons. Figs and pigs.
For Mopsus, the big winner, the bells go off
and the management sends him back home in a limo.
For Calchas, the last indignity—the bus
with the other losers. That's what did him in.

Cape Cod Beach

The flashing green light at the Wychmere jetty
seems in this fog to forget from time to time
its business—announcing where we are and the danger
the rocks pose at the harbor's entrance. The years
will bring to us all such moments, but I can remember
only too clearly glaring sun on this sand
where we spread our blankets, or sailing out there on the water,
blue years ago, but black and cold now, where a huge

fog bank looms twenty yards or so offshore
like some nocturnal predator with a taste
for happy times and places. Let it come
to devour at last what remains of this strip of beach,
children at play in that dazzling sun, and loss
for which it is stupid to think these waves still sigh.

Moses

If Moses could not enter, which of us can presume?

His offense was striking the rock. But where does it say
that to strike a rock is forbidden? And what harm did he do
to the rock, which, anyway, gave the precious water?
His defect, I fear, was more grave—an excess of goodness
that common sense would suggest is where we should look
in such a man, against whom, it is said, "the angels
banded together."
                              Because he had brought from heaven
the mighty mainstay, the Torah. His act did not
diminish heaven so much as elevate earth—
but still, from then on, the separation was less.

No ravening birds swarmed to tear at his liver
on a mountainside in the frozen north. Such stories,
too vivid, too violent, are not for us. But Jokhebed
cried aloud and looked in the valley of Moab
for the burial place, but it was nowhere to be seen.

She could not weep at his tomb, could not recite
the proper prayers, and her heart was sore, and in heaven
he knew, and cried aloud, "Jokhebed, my mother!"
loud and bitter, as if he were not in heaven,
as if there, too, he had not been permitted entrance.

Repetition

Somewhere between the rehearsals and reenactments
there must be—we suppose—a performance we either
perceive or whimsically choose and declare as the real

thing to which past and future, knowing or not,
all along referred. That welter of repetitions
turns out in the end not to have been so free,

as meaning imposes or, like the dumb sun, dawns,
and objects that swam in an indeterminate sea
of diffident potential assume their recalcitrant

shapes. So it is with events we thought we knew
rather too well. Beginnings and endings are clear,
but middles, that murk where significance often lurks,

are tricky, and joy, which ought to be easy enough
to recognize, defies the fastest tripping
shutter or eyelash flutter and, sly, furtive,

shy as a timid child, is abruptly gone,
leaving us searching, rummaging high and low
(those, I'm afraid, are the usual places), looking

for some faint trace or imprint. Exceptional moments?
Diversions, mostly. Experience, where we live,
is lying down each night, disposed the same way

on the same bedding we tidied that morning. The rumples
we smoothed mean more than the wretched or splendid dreams
our souls proposed while our bodies shifted or thrashed.

What's hard to see is whatever the blasé eye
assumes as we tread our daily round: a flash
of red as a cardinal crosses the sky, we'll remark,

looking up, and ignore how our path leads gently downward.

Falling from Silence

for Sam

Listening, listening, picking out sounds and phonemes,
patterns of vowels and consonants, objects and actions,
the words that up until now he has not required,
surrounded by babble, in constant cooing and crooning
he floats like a fish in the water or bird in the air,
swooping and soaring at play in an aether of love.